EMPLOY YOURSELF NOW
ENJOY YOURSELF NOW

7 STEPS TO START AND OPERATE A BUSINESS

IN LESS THAN 90 DAYS

Jack Terry, B.S. Bus., J.D.

For information: jterryaz007@gmail.com or
employ-yourself-now.com.

A Bikapelli Press Book, Published by Lightning Source, a subsidiary of
Ingram Press Publishers, 1246 Heil Quaker Blvd., LaVergne, Tennessee 37086

First Edition: Printed 2013

Formatting and Cover designed by: Launchpad Press, Cody, WY
www.launchpad-press.com

Library of Congress Cataloging-in-Publication Data has been applied for.

10 09 08 07 06 05 04 03 02 01

ISBN-13: 978-1-4839-3930-8 (Trade Paperback)

CONTENTS

REWARDS

Dedicated to all entrepreneurs—

and would-be entrepreneurs—in the greatest country

in the world, where you have the freedom to be

what you want to be.

God Bless America

INTRODUCTION

There are many books out there that offer an introduction to the world of business.

But you should ask yourself,

- What is the author's background?
- Was the author someone who just researched the subject?
- Was the author a teacher or professor who mostly gained knowledge from other books?
- Was the author someone who had only one or maybe two businesses?

WHAT MAKES MY BOOK UNIQUE, in comparison, is that I also tell my life story as a dedicated entrepreneur. I am passing on to you a lifetime of starting and operating over twenty businesses, each in a different field. I relate the excitement I have experienced—not only in the business, but also in the rewards with which I was able to indulge myself.

I started with very little. I then expanded the gains from the first business to the next business. Each success was compounded within another business. Of course, the compounding can also take place by growing your present business. Yet, be open minded to accepting an offer to buy your business (which may be a stepping stone to an even greater experience).

You, too, can have a life as exciting as I did. You just have to commit to taking the first step and believe in yourself.

Now, turn to the next page, not only of this book but also to begin a new chapter of your life.

The Unknown Can Be Scary

Not having a job is scary when you need one.

Looking at starting a business is scary if you have never done it.

The "scare" will disappear as you grasp and befriend the step-by-step basics listed here.

Expect to enjoy yourself now as you employ yourself now.

Step 1. Come up with a great idea.

Come up with an idea you can live with. I started my first business in my third year of college. My mom bought me enough hours of ballroom dance lessons that I eventually became a qualified instructor. I could have been satisfied to just be the best overall dancer at every dance I attended. But my intuition suggested I should put my ability to a better use and try to at least recover the money my mom had spent.

The college town didn't have a dance studio, so there was an opportunity waiting for someone to grab it and run with it. Basically I allowed my mind to capture what I heard, read, and observed around me.

Accept all thoughts and ideas. Mentally process them. Choose what you feel comfortable with and or have a passion for. Friends may offer their ideas for a business. Many of my ventures developed because I liked what another person offered or suggested. It isn't necessary that you be the creator of an idea that you grab onto and develop into a business.

Age is not a factor. A lady in her eighties started painting. Before she was ninety she was a multi-millionaire. A high school boy started selling office chairs at age fourteen. Now, in his mid-twenties, his sales are over $50 million. In another instance, a seventeen-year-old liked planning trips. Eventually he acquired busses and limousines to take customers on his planned trips. His revenues are now over $6 million. Startups like these required less than $100.

Chapter two was suggested by my high school friend. We were in our second year of law school. He envisioned building the largest golf driving range in Cleveland. Together we did it.

Another friend inspired the formation of chapter four. The business outlined in chapter five attracted me because my partner from chapter two was a stock broker at the time and encouraged me to join the same firm. I didn't own stock in the firm at the beginning, but I bought stock later. I became involved with the businesses in chapters eight through fourteen because of friendships established along the way. How? By getting involved in business groups, staying in touch with college friends, and meeting other stockbrokers.

My involvement with the business in chapter fifteen occurred three years before joining the operation My lady friend wanted to be in the business but couldn't finance the business on her own. I saw the potential in the business and decided to finance 50 percent of what the franchise required.

As you will notice, I only originated the businesses in chapter one and sixteen.

That is why it pays to make friends everywhere. Sometimes you can be invited to join a business because of what talents you have to offer; then you can acquire stock later.

Step 2. Establish a company name.

Have it describe what you are about to offer. "Jones Ventures"? What does that tell you about the business? Nothing! "Jones Bicycle Repair"? That is clear and everyone will understand what you have to offer. Here are some more clear examples.

- J. T. Dance Studio
- Stop 'n Swat Golf Driving Range
- Holiday Valley Ski Area
- Jim's Print Shop

One day I came across a very artistic and colorful sign above a business door in Honolulu. To this day I couldn't tell you what type of business they were in. As I drove by, I could not glance long enough to read the sign without getting into an accident.

Chapter nine was an exception. Torian's Plum, a restaurant, was written up in *Town & Country* as the finest restaurant in Steamboat Springs, Colorado, and had a following by movie stars such as Robert Redford and Ethyl Kennedy from the beginning.

Step 3. Location, location, location.

Location will depend upon what you plan to do and what you can afford. A high-traffic area, like in a shopping center or a busy corner location, costs more and is necessary if you want to open, say, a yogurt shop or a hamburger shop. But, if you can begin at home or in a garage, do so. Keep your overhead to a minimum in all possible areas.

When I started my first business (ballroom dance studio) I rented a second-floor storage space above a four-lane bowling alley. There was room for an office, two dance studio rooms and my living quarters. The rent was no more than I would have had to pay for an apartment in town. This meant zero overhead for the new business.

Step 4. Business setup.

If you are starting something alone, your organization will be a sole proprietorship. Considering taxes, you could begin using your present social security number and file a 1040 tax return form. Also, initially or sometime later, you could use a Subchapter S-corporation or a regular corporation to avoid personal liability. Discuss this with a qualified tax professional, preferably a Certified Public Accountant (CPA) or a tax lawyer.

If you will have one or more partners, then you will have a partnership agreement or a corporation created by your lawyer.

Step 5. Business banking.

Should I use a big bank or a small one? Quite often a small local bank will be the most friendly and go out of their way to be helpful. And they will be glad to have a new account, even if you are not a big operation. You will want checks (with your company name) and deposit slips. I can't remember not being warmly welcomed when opening a new account at a local bank. The ability to process credit cards may not be necessary at the beginning. With my first business I only accepted cash or checks. The business in chapter two was cash only, but the business in chapter sixteen required credit card capability from the beginning.

A few years ago, when I opened a business account for a limited liability corporation (LLC),the bank took my name and phone number and had a "business banker" call and make an appointment. That banker was very helpful and made sure everything was done properly.

Step 6. Establish a realistic budget.

A budget requires that you estimate each possible expense for each month for the next six months. List every expense you can imagine, down to the smallest item (such as postage stamps). List each expense separately. If this is foreign to you, ask your accountant or CPA for assistance. You could also take a bookkeeping course at a community college, or buy a book on basic bookkeeping.

For estimating income, do the best you can at guessing. Also, have a minimum amount you think possible for the first month, a little more for the second month, etc. Review your budget often—at first even weekly. This will enable you to anticipate when you should reach a break even point. An example of my budget is shown in chapter sixteen.

Now that you have your budget, you will need enough money to keep you going until you reach steady profitability. This can be obtained by adding together your monthly losses and profits for the first six months. The net loss represents your minimum financing required. I'd suggest at least doubling that amount. If your overhead is at a minimum, and you take little salary or no salary, you could be steadily profitable before the first six months have passed.

Never stop creating budgets. As you grow and expand, create an updated budget at least four times a year. This will allow you to anticipate future cash requirements to support your growth.

Be careful not to withdraw more money than your company can afford. There were some months I took no salary or a reduced salary. Even established businesses can have a slow month now and then. Also, you will need to plan the accumulation of funds for future equipment or inventory purchases.

Don't reduce your prices because of competition. You need to remain profitable. Let your competitor go out of business. Continue to be service oriented—customers will stay with you if they know you will go out of your way to please them. I remember one customer of my print shop (a personal friend) who said I should lower my prices or he would go across the street to a competitor. I explained to him that wasn't how I learned to run a business. I welcomed his decision to go across the street, and I told him I would also welcome him if he came back. In a couple months he returned. He didn't like the way he was treated at the other shop.

Step 7. Showtime!

Now it's up to you to put it all in play.

Only you can accomplish your dream.

Precursors

Robert Goddard, *Physicist,* **was the first to develop a liquid-fuel rocket. He is quoted as saying, "Every vision is a joke until the first man accomplishes it; once realized, it becomes commonplace."**

You have a choice: work for yourself or someone else. Choose whatever works best with your temperament and your goals. I have found more satisfaction working for myself. Only YOU can accomplish your dream.

Back when I was about four or five years old, I started with a small lemonade stand table on the sidewalk in front of my childhood home. Mom made the lemonade and I sat behind the table with a sign that read "Lemonade—1 cent per glass."

Some of my playmates borrowed a penny from a parent in order to purchase a glass. Even people in passing cars would stop to have their thirst quenched (and help out a young entrepreneur). It was the mid-1930s; everyone seemed friendlier and more trusting, and everything moved at a much slower pace.

During my early teen years I had a newspaper route for at least three years and cut lawns until I was a senior in high school.

When in my freshman year in high school, Louis (a school friend and neighbor) and I decided to produce and sell something we called a "Cap & BB Bomb" in high school. No, it wasn't really a "bomb"; rather, it was a BB (copper or steel) that was covered with a cap (cut from a roll of caps used in a cap pistol), and then covered with a square of cellophane. The cellophane was twisted together at all four corners to form a tail. The cap was at the opposite end. When thrown into the air or against something hard, the cap would pop.

Back then caps sold for one cent per roll of fifty. We obtained the cellophane from bread loaf wrappers. Louis and I each made 100 the first night and sold them the next day at school. We began with an initial price of four for a penny. The product sold so well that I changed the price to two for a penny the next day. Then I dropped the price to one for a penny because they were selling so well. I guess you would call that 'pricing a product or service according to the demand'.

On my fourth day in business, I sold my 100 early in the morning. Unfortunately our 'customers' got a little too creative. Some of our Cap & BB products were dropped off the balcony during the noon movie. One student threw one at a blackboard during class. Of course, this could not continue.

The principal called me into his office after lunch, and there was Louis unwrapping the products he had not sold. We were then placed on a bench in the reception office and told to sit there until it was time to go home. We were also told that the police would show up at our respective homes and talk to our parents.

While sitting on the hard office bench, Louis and I heard the teachers talking with each other as they came in and went out. They had no idea who we were or why we were there. One teacher exclaimed to the other, "Did you hear about the two boys who were selling *hand grenades?*" We looked at each other and smiled.

I got home the usual time (three-thirty to four p.m.). I said nothing to Mom regarding the day's events. My dad got home about five p.m. A police car pulled up in front of our house at about five-forty-five. I rushed to Dad and quickly relayed what had happened that day at school. He said, "Just relax; I'll talk to the policeman."

Time passed slowly as I waited. After about twenty minutes (though it seemed like twenty hours) Dad came back into the house. I was imagining the worst. Dad walked toward me, put his hand on my shoulder, and said, "Son, you're quite a businessman!" and walked away to see what was for dinner.

Why did it end that way? Perhaps because I was an otherwise good student, and Dad created some minor concerns himself when he was in high school. From what I could tell, he was glad I wasn't a milk toast kid. But I did learn quickly the unpleasantness that comes from creating mischief, and that I ultimately had to take responsibility for it. It was a bit too much stress, even then.

In the ensuing chapters, you will notice that I held ownership in all but one or two of the ventures reviewed.

You will see:

1. how patience vs. exhibiting anger can pay big dividends. Learn to control your emotions as best you can.
2. how many unexpected challenges and "road blocks" will arise to test your ability to respond, adjust, and overcome.
3. that not everyone has the fortitude to continue overcoming the daily business challenges as a way of life, even though the rewards can be well worth the effort.
4. when it comes to "challenges", sometimes an employee can be listed in this category.

I have also found that it pays to:

a. be curious.
b. make friends—everywhere.
c. be a team player.
d. always operate at a "level 10."
e. be *very* careful in whom you trust.
f. be alert; know what service or product a customer may need.
g. do not give up if you experience a loss now and then.
h. take responsibility for your actions.
i. be able to read an accounting statement. Take a class. You need to be able to tell if you are making a profit or loss. If you are experiencing a loss, what can you cut out to get to a profit?
j. know in advance everything you can learn about any business you plan to enter. How? Read as much as you can find. Google or Bing the business. If there is a similar business nearby, go inside and observe. Better yet, get a part-time or full-time job in that business. Of course, you could buy a franchise and they will train you, but not everyone can afford to start that way.
k. become aware of your intuition and learn to trust it. There is a saying: "Intuition can lead to institution," meaning simply that you can follow your intuition and build a successful business.
l. Realize that operating your own business is not the same as an eight-hour-a-day, five-day-a-week job. Be prepared to give as much time as your business demands.
m. Always be engaged in the learning process. Explore. Listen. Read. Travel.

Next comes **Rewards**! Don't forget to treat yourself after an accomplishment. For a modest win, give yourself a modest reward. For a major win, give yourself a greater reward.

If you are an employee, let's hope your boss recognizes accomplishments. If you are the boss, rewards for a job well done can bring about more enthusiastic effort in the future.

In some of the chapters I'll describe how I rewarded my employees and between some of the chapters I will describe how I rewarded myself.

One more item before you open your business: spend conservatively. I've observed several startups where the owner(s) spent over 50 percent, in some cases even up to 80 percent, of their capital on fancy offices. Soon after, they wondered why they failed. Fancy offices don't pay the bills. Be protective toward your cash and conservative as to how you spend it.

Passion: "The road to happiness lies in two simple principles: find what interests you and that you can do well, and put your whole soul into it—every bit of energy and ambition and natural ability you have."
—**John D. Rockefeller,** *Oil Executive*

"Some see private enterprise as a predatory target to be shot – others as a cow ready to be milked. But few are those who see it as a sturdy horse pulling the wagon."
—**Winston Churchill,** *Former British Prime Minister*

Chapter 1

Ballroom Dance Studio

It was 1947, I was seventeen, and ready to graduate from high school. My father had passed away one year earlier when he was forty-five years old. My mother, a very aware person, had heard of new psychological test designed to determine the direction that a person should take in his or her career. She encouraged me to take the test, but I was not happy with the results. The test determined for me that I didn't have the innate ability to do much more than be an accountant or bookkeeper. I had always wanted to be an aeronautical engineer. Because of the disappointing test results, I put all hopes of engineering aside and opened up to whatever would come next.

In hindsight, it is obvious that the psychologists didn't know what they were doing. I ended up accomplishing more than they ever thought possible.

Don't let others distract you from your goals, or tell you that you cannot do something. Pay attention to your passions. Follow your passions when it comes to developing a business idea or, at the very least, consider filling a need that isn't currently offered in your community. A good example of this is Bill Lear of the Lear Jet Corporation. He had an eight-grade-level education but he ended up filing over 150 patents throughout his lifetime.

I wasn't sure what I was going to do about college. I took a job as a secretary, tasked with taking notations in shorthand and typing, in a two-man sales office for a year after graduation from high school. During that time my mom bought me fifty-five hours of dance lessons at the Arthur Murray Dance Studio in Cleveland. A friend of hers said that I would have more fun in college. Her friend was right.

I started attending college at Miami University in Oxford, Ohio, the very

1

next year. And I had attended my first ballroom dance about two months after school started. I was surprised that I was the only freshman male who knew how to dance—and properly lead a partner. The women noticed this immediately and would line up five or ten deep in order to dance…with me! That was a confidence-building experience I'll never forget. And it continues to occur wherever I go dancing.

After my first year in college, I asked Mom for more dance lessons. She is willing and supportive. I took the next 140 hours of ballroom dance class time at the Fred Astaire Studio in Cleveland during the summer. I was offered a special price for the hours: the entire package would be refunded if I didn't advance to their or our satisfaction. I completed the course that summer with the praise of my teachers.

Knowledge of the basic and intermediate dance steps in both American and Latin dances qualified me to get a part-time teaching position at the Fred Astaire dance studio in Cincinnati. This helped with some of my college costs and allowed me to have a car on campus. And, with that experience, I learned how to promote and operate a dance studio. I obtained copies of lesson plans and pricing packages. Now I could budget costs and project income and expenses.

Of course projections are guesses. But continue to review what you list first. Then review it again and again. Be conservative. You'll be surprised how close you can get to actual results. See more about budgeting in Chapter 16.

My desire to participate in college social life found me joining the cross-country track team and playing tennis. I joined the Reserve Officers' Training Corps (ROTC) to assure that I would not be drafted before finishing school. In my second year of college, I joined the Freshman Manual committee as business manager of the "M-Book" and was business manager for the campus humor magazine, "The Tomahawk."

At the end of my second college year, I discovered the need for and a public interest in a dance studio in my college town of Oxford, Ohio. I rented the second floor of a two-story building in "uptown" Oxford. There were four bowling lanes on the first floor. The second floor, at the top of the stairs, had a wall dividing the area: one-third in the front and two-thirds in the back. My interest was in the dusty, empty back two-thirds. The flooring was wood (ideal for dancing). To minimize costs, I strung steel wires from front to back and side to side and hung fabric, instead of building walls, to cut down on costs. This created four rooms. The fabric was on sale and very colorful (actually gray with gaudy, bright, colorful patterns) with the weight similar to furniture covering. I now had an office, living quarters (with the mattress on the floor) and two dance studio rooms. I located a desk and several chairs at a garage sale, and painted the weight bearing walls. The cost of living somewhere else in town was almost equal to the rent I paid for the entire dance studio space. This setup represented an almost zero overhead to start my business.

From the beginning, business was good. In fact, I had to stop advertising after two months. I did advertise in the local paper for part-time female dance teachers who lived in town and who had taught at major dance studios earlier in their lives. Luckily I found two. I was anticipating having to teach one or two women before they would be able to teach at the studio. As a result, the studio could operate while I was attending classes. I also added another teacher (Jane) to teach tap, acrobatic, and ballet to local children. She was my fraternity brother's girlfriend.

Business not only was good, but also with two years of business coming to a close, as well as my senior year, I was about two months from graduation. What do I do with the business? Should I remain in Oxford and operate the dance studio or sell the dance studio? In the end neither choice was available. Why? The building burned down. Fortunately I was not in the building, but I was at the fraternity house. A fraternity brother came running in and frantically said, "Your dance studio is on fire." Since that was about the seventh time I was told about a fire at my dance studio when the uptown volunteer fire siren blared, my response was "Yeah, yeah, I've heard that before." "No, really," he said in a pleading manner. I immediately went uptown; this time the studio was really on fire.

The fire was accidently caused by a kerosene deliveryman from the Standard Oil Company of Ohio (SOHIO). SOHIO settled for about $3,000, and I received about $1,000 from my homeowners' insurance. Sixty years later (2012), this $4,000 would exceed $60,000 due to inflation.

This business was a sole proprietorship (meaning I was the sole owner). This is the easiest way to operate (even though all the decision making is on your shoulders, and there is greater personal liability if the venture fails). In chapter two, there are three partners and transparency and honest communication become essential.

Critique

After graduation, I attended three job interviews: NCR, Kodak, and Marathon Paper. They all offered me an accounting job. I said no thanks. I wanted something more exciting, like sales, but I was turned down. (If only they could have experienced my success in Chapter 21.) I decided to go to law school because of my business law professor. He made the practice of law sound exciting. How fortunate to have had a teacher who made a class that dynamic.

"Do you know the difference between education and experience? Education is when you read the fine print; experience is what you get when you don't."
—Pete Seeger, *Musician*

On Learning: "The thing that's important to know is that you never know. You're always sort of feeling your way."
—Diane Arbus, *Photographer*

Reward 1

After the success of the business listed in chapter one, my high school friend Elmer and I decided to spend three or four summer weeks of 1952 driving to Florida in his Studebaker. We stopped and visited many college campuses between Cleveland and Miami.

We entered northern Florida on a bright Sunday morning. Around nine a.m. we drove into a small town with the speedometer reading 15 miles per hour. Suddenly there was a police car behind us with siren blaring and all lights blinking. I pulled to the side of the road at the police officer's direction. When asked for my driver's license, I asked, "Why were we pulled over?" His response: "Speeding." "But I did not exceed 15 miles per hour," I said. The officer said the speed limit was 10 miles per hour and the sign was back where we had entered the town.

Upon arriving at the police station, the officer reaches for the car keys as I am giving them to Elmer. I explained that the car was Elmer's. The fine was $35. This equates to $500 about fifty years later. I resisted making payment, and was locked in an old jail cell with a flop-down bed and a cigarette-burned mattress. Elm met me at the barred jail window and said he would find the mayor and complain. Forty-five minutes later Elm returns with bad news. The mayor is twenty-seven years old. He said if we want to contest the fine, we would have to come back in three days for the trial.

We learned that you couldn't fight a Florida speed trap; we paid the fine and continued our trip. Actually, we were lucky we only got caught by one speed trap.

Soon we were in Orlando. I saw a sign for water ski lessons; I wanted to learn. The owner of the lake and the ski school was Mr. Suydam. He was a champion water skier; his son eventually held the same title. After instructions from Mr. S on the beach, we are up and skiing side by side around the lake. Amazingly, I caught on with my first attempt. I pay 50 cents for a couple more trips around the lake. Then it was on to South Florida.

In Miami I paid for one more water ski ride. At $5 that was enough. On our way north, I asked Elm to stop at Mr. S's lake again so I could take a lesson on one ski. Again, I succeeded on the first try. But I also had my first fall when I was not paying attention. As Mr. S turned the boat around, he saw me thrashing in the water. "Don't you know how to swim?" "No," I said. "Okay, get a hold of the ski, put it on, place the other foot behind, and press against the water as I get up to speed." I was up and able to return on one ski. I was as surprised as anyone that I actually got up on one ski. By the way, life jackets weren't provided in those days.

"Investment decisions or personal decisions don't wait for the picture to be clarified."
—**Andrew Grove,** *Executive*

Chapter 2

Golf Driving Range

The summer after my college graduation I reconnected with Elmer, a high school friend who also just graduated but from an out-of-state college.

Elmer was very interested in the stock market, and suggested I meet with his broker at Merrill Lynch. The meeting was congenial and I invested $3,000 of my "fire money" with this broker. Then we drove to Florida from Cleveland for the summer break.

At the end of the summer, Elm and I enrolled in law school at Case Western Reserve University (in Cleveland, Ohio). By the middle of our second year, Elm decided to drop out of law school and become a stock broker (he remained a stock broker for the rest of his working life). I continued law school.

During the summer before my third year of law school, Elm suggested we build a golf driving range. I liked the idea and saw the need for a really first-class golf practice center. Elm was a very good golfer, having played on his high school and college golf teams.

Initially we visited every golf driving range on the west side of Cleveland to understand what was available. We made notes on what we liked and what we didn't like at each range. Next we recorded the pricing for a bucket of balls and the hours of operation. Then we spoke to other golfers to learn what they would like to find in the "ideal" range. We also received bids on construction. This indicated the need for additional funds up to $100,000.

By then my $3,000 investment at Merrill Lynch had grown to over $7,000. Elm and I agreed to each invest $7,000 into a new corporation, which would build and own the golf driving range. However, this wasn't enough to properly start the project. Elm brought in his friend Tom to add another $7,000. And he was someone who could loan up to another $100,000 to the venture. Now the funding was complete. Each of us owned one-third of the corporation, plus Tom would receive a note for his loan (later determined to be $70,000) with an agreed upon rate of interest.

Prior to the final depositing of the funds into the corporation, it became urgent to us that we draft and execute an agreement to cover whatever might happen in our lives and the life of the corporation. Each of us contributed our ideas for personal and corporate protection. After the initial draft, we had our personal attorneys review it and make their suggestions. By the time the final agreement was signed, I thought it was amazingly thorough. Not only was every imaginable circumstance covered but, by the end of this venture, every clause was utilized and the end result was rewarding to all parties.

Land had to be located. Here is where my two completed years of law school started to pay off. Going through plat maps—to-scale maps showing the divisions of a piece of land—I located two side-by-side lots on a main thoroughfare that seemed ideal for our purpose. Then I went to each owner with an *option to purchase** agreement, including a non-refundable deposit if we did not complete the purchase. Otherwise, the deposit would be applied to the purchase price. (* see glossary)

One owner, Mr. A, was very willing to sell. Owner Mr. B was difficult. He wasn't prepared to sell. But, when he realized that he could keep the deposit if we did not purchase the lot, he relented. He felt sure I could not get a rezoning and he would be ahead the amount of the binding deposit.

A neighbor who lived across the street from me named Bob was a vice president of the bank that had a branch in the community where I would argue the rezoning. Bob introduced me personally to the manager of this branch. This was critical. I learned that two members of the five-member zoning board would vote against me and two would approve my request. Success depended upon the fifth member, Gil. The branch manager told me that Gil had a side business of selling and constructing outdoor grills. As you might assume, I became *very* interested in outdoor grills. I couldn't ask Gil enough about the business, how he had gotten into that business, what the price range was for his grills, how long it took to design and build. Also, of course, I thought such a grill might fit well at the driving range.

The zoning board meeting was a week later. After my presentation, the board voted three to two in my favor. It sure helped to know the interests of the board members.

Then it was time to get purchase agreements drafted and signed. Again, seller Mr. A was easy to work with. Seller Mr. B? Well, he wanted his money in thirty days. That was tight timing for us since Tom was in the process of transferring the $70,000. So, I had to utilize my contract drafting skills. This was easy with Mr. A; I created a one-page document. For Mr. B I drafted a three-page agreement. Page one agreed to a thirty-day payment. Page two was commentary (also known as "boilerplate"). Page three was worded in such a way that allowed an extension of another thirty days… indirectly and depending upon other circumstances. Seller B's attorney read and approved the agreement. Always hire an attorney if you are not legally trained.

We did have to extend the payment and closing a couple weeks beyond the first thirty days. Seller Mr. B had a slight tantrum, but everything closed within the second thirty days. By this time, I had graduated from law school.

Time to construct our driving range. We had purchased a total of twenty-eight acres on a main thoroughfare. **Stop 'n Swat Golf Driving Range** would become the largest in Cleveland with forty-one tees—ten tees covered for bad weather—a small club house, powerful high pole night lights, and an eighteen-hole miniature golf course.

A law school classmate was already a civil engineer and he agreed to survey our property for development. It was necessary to move a lot of earth to give golfers a clear view of the terrain and get proper run off of rain water. All earth moving was finished before winter's arrival.

In January 1956 I was drafted into the Army. Suppliers and installers had already been researched and selected. During 1956 and 1957 my partners supervised the completion of the Stop 'n Swat Golf Driving Range, club house, miniature golf course, driveway, and tall pole flood lights.

Advertising and promotion was minimal since we now owned over 200 feet of frontage on a busy main street. Soon after the land purchase was completed, we erected a sign at our entrance: "Coming Soon: Stop 'n Swat Golf Driving Range." As we finished construction, the sign changed to "Opening Spring 1958." Finally, we were open, and our customers arrived. Also, as I recall, we ran some ads in the sports section of the local papers announcing the opening.

I was discharged in December 1957 after serving in Germany. Stop 'n Swat opened in the spring of 1958. Business was outstanding from the beginning, even on rainy days, because of the covered tees. Three golf professionals made themselves available for lessons, and they kept whatever they charged for their lessons. One "pro" said to me "Jack, your swing needs some help." I laughed to myself. It sure did, and I received several lessons.

Near the end of the summer, we were contacted by homebuilders. They wanted our twenty-eight acres and were offering prices we could not ignore. The sale took place. My share was $20,000—almost a triple return on my original $7,000 investment.

Reward 3

According to **Napoleon Bonaparte**, *the French Emperor,* "Riches do not consist in the possession of treasures, but in the use made of them."

With that thought in mind, I called my car dealer friends in Nuremberg, Germany, and ordered a new Porsche. The color would be a medium green with tan leather interior. When this special order was delivered to my friends in Nuremberg, I flew there to pick it up. That evening, my friends took me to dinner, with a stop first at the home of friends of theirs. This home was large and represented a very wealthy family. I was treated to some schnapps while getting acquainted. Before leaving for the restaurant, the man of the home offered me either of his daughters in marriage for 100,000 German marks (equal to $25,000 then and about $375,000 fifty years later). The girls were ages seventeen and nineteen, and neither appealed to me. So I said I needed time to consider his offer, and off we went to dinner.

A couple days later, I'm off on a two-month driving tour of Europe, including a stop in London. This required a ferryboat crossing of the English Channel. I overnighted in a Brussels, Belgium, hotel. Arising at six a.m. and paying my bill, I asked the front desk clerk if my selected ferryboat left on time. After looking at my schedule, he said, "No, that ferry doesn't sail this time of year, but here is one that does." In fact, it was scheduled to leave in one hour and ten minutes. "And what is the distance to the dock?" I asked. "About 100 miles," he said. Again I asked, "Is it a good road?" "Yes, straight all the way." I rushed to my Porsche and took off. What a car. I arrived at the port in one hour flat (with ten minutes to spare), hitting a high speed of 118 miles per hour. It was legal there.

Once on the ferryboat, I ordered lunch and a martini. When the martini arrived, it was brown. Upon inquiring, I discovered that they use sweet vermouth in Europe instead of dry vermouth. The waiter quickly made the change. I spent four days in London, but I did not drive my car when I got there. Driving on the left side of the road in the busy city of London was more than I wanted to contend with. Also, the taxis were inexpensive. A lady friend I met on the cruise ship going to Europe became my tour guide around London. Next, it was back to Amsterdam to ship the car home.

Now, with the car safely on its way back to America, I followed through on Henry Brada's invitation (see Reward 2) to visit him in Helsinki. Dates were scheduled for almost every night during my two weeks there. I even went cross-country skiing in Lapland (northern Finland) where the sun came up at eleven a.m. and set at two p.m. (in November). Afterward, Henry took me to the Order of the Bath/Sauna-Seura. This must be one of a kind. Even *Reader's Digest* wrote a several-page article on it in its June 1968 issue. In between being "boiled" in three different steam rooms, you are massaged, scrub-washed, and leaf-branch switched. Then we went outside and jumped in the Finish lake, which was about 33 degrees. I was out of the lake in about twelve seconds. Then I was directed to relax on a bed for twenty to thirty minutes so that my nervous system could get somewhere back to normal. Then I was awarded a certificate (10" x 18 ") confirming me as a "Knight of the Sauna." The powerful rush of energy experienced afterward lasted for two weeks.

For the last month, I had been receiving telegrams from a friend named Donald. He had a new business venture and was anxious for me to return and help finance it.

Some years later (when I was with the stock brokerage firm) Henry would visit me in Cleveland, to learn about corporate stockholder battles to control a corporation.

Critique

In retrospect, I never contemplated that I could **not** do what I planned. I only concentrated on what it would take to get *the* job done—whatever *the* was.

"The most rewarding things you do in life are often the ones that look like they cannot be done."
—**Arnold Palmer,** *Golfer*

"Yesterday is a cancelled check. Tomorrow is a promissory note. Today is the only cash you have, so spend it wisely."
—**Kim Lyons,** *Athlete*

"Accept the challenges so that you may feel the exhilaration of victory."
—**George Patton,** *General*

"Face reality as it is, not as it was or as you wish it to be."
—**Jack Welch,** *General Electric CEO*

CHAPTER 3

OFFICERS' CLUB

Receiving my draft notice at twenty-six didn't seem to fit into my plans when I was in the middle of planning the golf driving range. One could call it a bad slice on a narrow fairway.

I arrived in Fort Leonard Wood, Missouri, called the "Hell Hole" by the draftees accompanying me. The other draftees were mostly seventeen or eighteen years old, and spoke among themselves as though they knew how to get to a preferred training base. I felt lost and just followed directions. And, to my pleasant surprise, they sent me to Camp Carson in Colorado Springs, Colorado.

Because of my typing skills, I became the company clerk. My responsibility was to file a "Morning Report," reporting everything that happened each prior day on a form using cryptic military abbreviations. This turned out to be a good assignment because my basic training was limited, taking second place to the "Morning Report." My rank: private.

After six months, my regiment was shipped to Germany. There were approximately 2,000 soldiers on this somewhat small ship crossing the North Atlantic in October, sleeping in hammocks stacked four high. One day, as I looked out a port hole, I could see that a wave was topping out above the smokestack of the ship. Ninety-nine percent of the people on board became sea sick at one point or other, including the crew. I survived by mentally being elsewhere.

Arriving in Hamburg, Germany, after about seven days onboard the ship, we transferred to a train that took us to Nuremberg in south central Germany. I totally enjoyed the train ride while passing through villages and towns while marveling at the architecture. It was a lush country with trees, farms, and vineyards everywhere. Our destination was Furth, a suburb of Nuremberg, and our final destination was an old Luftwaffe air base.

I heard that the colonel of the regiment was looking for a regimental stenographer. I took a shorthand course in high school at the urging of my typing teacher. I was the only male in the class and felt out of place at the time. Little did I realize then that shorthand would totally change my military experience. I applied.

I got the job. I became the colonel's secretary and the regimental stenographer. In this position, I became aware of everything going on at headquarters. I met the new Officers' Club officer. After telling him I had worked for a CPA while attending law school, this captain told me of the bad administrative condition of the "O Club." I offered to audit it. The colonel gave his blessing, knowing I'd only be a couple buildings away if he needed me for steno work.

The Officers' Club was a two-story building with sleeping accommodations for about sixteen officers, a dining room, bar lounge, large party room, administrative offices, a living room type of entrance, and a full kitchen. Behind were two tennis courts.

My audit was complete in about three weeks. Everything that could be wrong was wrong.

a. too many employees in the office.
b. food and bar repricing hadn't been adjusted for cost increases.
c. the two sergeants running the club weren't collecting dues from the officers.
d. the two waitresses were bitchy most of the time.
e. the two sergeants were sleeping with the waitresses, which gave them the feeling they couldn't be fired, no matter what.
f. club was losing money every month.

After reporting this information to my superiors, I recommended replacing the management and volunteered myself. The colonel totally approved of the suggestions, and Private Terry became Manager of the Officers' Club. I moved into the Club in an officer's room. I am now wearing civilian clothes most of the time and have the freedom to plan my day as necessary—but always available for the colonel's needs. The sergeants were reassigned to another base in Germany (but not without first threatening my life). The waitresses were given a choice: resign and apply elsewhere or be placed on a military no-hire list. They resigned. The other employees were very happy with the changes, and took a renewed pride in their work. In order to get into town to purchase supplies, I bought a car—a 1938 Opel that survived World War II—for $125.

For me, this was like operating my own country club... without owning it. Within a couple of months the club's character had completely changed, and it showed a profit every month thereafter. As John Wooden, *basketball coach,* once said: "Respect a man, and he will do all the more."

A month or two later (on a Saturday morning), I received a call from the other officers' club in Nuremberg. They had mistakenly booked two generals' parties for that evening, and they asked if I would take one. Most of my employees were off for the weekend. I said I would call the employees and get back to them within an hour. Because of the respectful way I treated my employees, everyone came in to work this big party.

Nuremberg Officers' Club delivered the food we would need to prepare. My club artist/decorator/sign painter Werner gave the club a total party atmosphere. Whitey, the bartender, made sure we had enough booze. His wife, Resi, now one of the waitresses, and Richard, another private I hired as waiter and part-time accountant, set up the party room to handle the 100 or so guests expected that evening. Richard's uncle owned a hotel in NYC and he was an experienced waiter. The chef (Pete) and his helpers had the kitchen buzzing. I learned quickly how to mix drinks behind the bar with Whitey's guidance.

The event was an amazing success. The general's aide tipped me $20 (equal to over $300 fifty years later). I asked if it was permissible to accept the tip. The aide said the general had suggested it. I shared the tip with my employees. And more accolades were to come. The general sent a letter of commendation to me through all channels, including my colonel and the Club Officer.

American Express Travel offered special packaged trips to the soldiers in Europe. I bought one for $25—round-trip bus fare from Nuremberg to Paris for New Year's 1957, two nights hotel, one half-day tour of Paris (including the Louvre museum), and a bottle of champagne. At midnight on New Year's Eve, another soldier and I were walking around Place Pigalle (nicknamed "Pig Alley" by Allied soldiers during World War II because this is where the prostitutes operated). All bars and nightspots were filled with patrons. About 12:20 a.m., after the bells stopped ringing, a prostitute saw us walking down the street, opened the night club door and said "SFTF." My friend said, "Shall we go?" "No, I'll go back to the hotel," I said. My friend went with her and I cautiously returned to the hotel. The streets were quiet and mostly vacant at this time. I walked the middle of each street (not the sidewalks), always looking over my shoulder. I was ready to run if anyone came my way. It wasn't the most fun way to celebrate New Year's Eve, but it was another of life's experiences.

After selling my Opel to a captain for $150, I bought a new Volkswagen for about $900. The Army would pay to ship one car home, and I didn't really want to keep a 1938 Opel (ha).

It is now the summer of 1957, and I have two weeks of leave time to use or lose. Another friend, Manfred Belmore, born in Rome of English parents, worked for Siemens, a company similar to General Electric in America. His job was to translate the operating manuals for all of Siemens's products into every European language, including English. Manfred is what I would consider one brilliant human being.

Manfred suggested an outline for the two-week trip to utilize my leave time. From Nuremberg, we would drive through Switzerland (stopping in Zurich and Lucerne), the southern one-third of France, stopping in Biarritz. Until the 1950s it was the Monte Carlo of the Atlantic coast, transformed by Napoleon III during the mid-nineteenth century into a playground for monarchs, aristos, and glitterati. Next we would travel to Spain to visit Madrid and Barcelona. Then we would return to France via the southern coast, travel to the Riviera and Monaco, pass through northern Italy and western Austria, and then return to Nuremberg. My new VW is now ready to depart.

Once we started this trip, Manfred was like a private tour guide. Not only did he speak all the languages, he could explain the architecture of every church, castle, and edifice; when they were built; and when the Romans battled in these areas.

In Barcelona I used a letter of introduction from Richard to meet Gustavo Gili. He was very wealthy, owning large printing companies in Spain and Argentina. He collaborated with Picasso in printing his paintings in a limited edition book.

Only 1,000 were printed and, instead of money changing hands, each kept 500 books which could be sold sometime in the future. You can see one of these books in the Picasso Museum in Barcelona.

Mr. Gili offered to have my Volkswagen serviced at his dealership. Then he arranged for his son and his son's fiancée to take us out in the evening to a flamenco night club. I had never witnessed a more dynamic exhibition of the flamenco dance, and not a single tourist was in the audience—just well-to-do Spaniards. Richard and his father were very influential. (Another time I was able to stay in Prince Hohenlohe's condo in Munich, thanks to Richard.)

The next day we attended a genuine bullfight. Some people appreciate the skill involved, and some don't. I was enthralled by the entire spectacle: the crowd, the atmosphere, the noise, and the colors worn by attendees as well as the bull fighter. I was heartened to know that each killed bull was immediately butchered and the meat distributed to the poor. Next we drove along the southern coast of France, stopping to have lunch in a restaurant on the Riviera beach. There were bikinis everywhere. In Monaco we found the casino was closed due to a religious celebration. I was looking forward to "depositing" a few dollars there. In Italy we visited the Leaning Tower of Pisa. Manfred found a way to climb *above* the bells! He did the same in the spires of the Familia Church in Barcelona. When the Familia Church spires are finished, they will be the tallest in the world.

We were going through Austria on our way back to Germany. I had to do all 2,700 miles of the driving because Manfred (as I analyzed it) was so brilliant, his brain couldn't stay on one subject very long—in this case, a simple roadway. He was always pointing: "Look at that church," "Look at that museum," and so on. The same occurred in a park in Barcelona. He begged to drive just in the park. Soon after he was pointing and accidently drove up on the sidewalk.

I became a member of the Army regimental tennis team. In college I played on (and helped manage) the tennis team. With the military team I would go to different resorts, such as Stuttgart and Garmisch-Partenkirchen, for a week at a time to compete. In the finals (fall 1957) I received a trophy for runners-up in doubles in an all-Europe military tennis tournament. With this little bit of success, I was invited to play at some private German tennis clubs. For me this was a special award in itself. What surprised me most at these private tennis clubs was their beverage of choice: a mixture that was half lemonade and half beer. Very refreshing.

It was December 1957 and I was scheduled to be discharged soon. My colonel, the regimental commander, called me in for a meeting. He had just been appointed to be in charge of counterintelligence for the U. S. Army in all of Europe, and asked me to join him as his personal aide (replete with an officers' rank). This was a surprise offer that I least expected. *What an exciting opportunity*, I thought. But, the golf driving range had just been completed and was ready to open in about four months. That was another decision in the fork in the road of life. With deep apology and appreciation, I picked the driving range since I had most of my money invested there. The colonel understood and wished me well.

The Officers' Club was the one business I did not have any ownership in, but I operated it as though I did. The rewards were beyond my expectations.

On Achievement: "Be a yardstick of quality. Some people aren't used to an environment where excellence is expected."
—Steve Jobs, *Apple Co-founder*

On Experience: "Big jobs usually go to the men who prove their ability to outgrow small ones."
—Theodore Roosevelt, *26th U. S. President*

Reward 2

Now discharged from the Army and having my new Volkswagen, I drove to Florida with my mother in February 1958. How surprised I was to experience 34 miles per gallon of gas. My mother's sisters were vacationing in Tampa, and this gave her a chance to vacation with them.

In the Tampa area I met Henry (Jouku) Brada from Helsinki, Finland. He had just finished two years at UCLA and was returning home. A lifelong and rewarding friendship developed, including an invitation to visit him in Finland. I had no idea when I would be able to visit Finland, but it was much closer than I could have imagined.

On taking chances: "You've got to seize the opportunity if it is presented to you."
—**Clive Davis,** *Record Producer*

CHAPTER 4

ACCOUNTING, BILLING, AND COLLECTIONS

FOR DOCTORS AND DENTISTS

This chapter starts in Europe (as you will see in Reward 2).

A friend of mine (Donald M.) had been telegraphing me with a business idea he felt had much potential: providing accounting and billing services to the medical profession. The year was 1958, and such services were in their infancy. This was before computers as we know them in the twenty-first century.

Don sold insurance to the medical profession very successfully and understood their other needs, such as accounting and billing services, but he also wanted to simplify their office procedures by taking these services outside of their office. He had researched the type of equipment available to do the service. He located a mature woman in her forties who also had an extensive accounting background to operate the equipment. I interviewed the lady, and agreed she was ideal for the job.

We decided upon a partnership, with profits and ownership to be split right down the middle. I would loan the company $10,000 in return for a note at an agreed upon rate of interest. This amount would be more than enough to buy the equipment—a National Cash Register (NCR) bookkeeping machine with the appearance of a typewriter and a 30-plus–inch carriage—as well as provide working capital, a deposit for the office space, and many months' salary for our one employee. We named the company M/T Systems... the first letter of our last names. Below this short name, we added "Accounting and Billing Services for the Medical Profession."

Don would handle the outside sales calls. I would assist wherever needed. A legal agreement was drafted to cover our personal and family interests, and it was approved by our respective attorneys.

Don already had several clients ready to go. One was the leading surgeon in Cleveland and another was one of the most respected family doctors in Cleveland. They both agreed to use our services, be our centers of influence, and recommend other doctors to our service.

After Don described how the doctors would be billed, I worked up potential income and expense projections. The figures looked good. Neither Don nor I would take a salary. He had a good income from insurance sales. We would look ahead to sharing the profits.

In addition to providing accounting, billing, and collection services, Don felt we could also handle their insurance and investment needs. Don was already licensed to sell insurance, so I joined a brokerage firm to get a securities license. This would provide my regular income.

It was time to market M/T Systems. The task seemed like a walk in the park with Don's contacts and our two main centers of influence. But, as **Yogi Berra** said, "Predictions are tough—especially about the future." And so it was!

With the business under way and the future looking great, we received bad news. The surgeon suffered a detached retina and the family doctor had a heart attack. So went our main referral pool. Both docs were disabled for many months.

Was this a coincidence? Maybe not.

Don was still upbeat. I was concerned. The bookkeeper could see a bright future even though this was a bump in the road. She offered me a return of my $10,000 from her own savings. I accepted and became a full-time stock broker. The parting was very cordial. M/T Systems continued successfully for many years thereafter.

Reward 4

In between chapters four and five (1959), I returned to Germany for a couple weeks. I visited friends and past employees of the Officers' Club. I also picked up another Volkswagen Bug. I had sold the Porsche for $200 more than I had invested in it. Why? I was so busy with the business listed in chapter four that I wasn't driving it much, and someone offered me a good price. After shipping the VW home from Amsterdam, I returned by plane to Cleveland.

That year I joined the Cleveland Ski Club and met Dick Bohr. Dick was among those who were initially involved in planning the Vail, Colorado, ski area. Now he planned to open a ski sports store to be named "Ski Haus." I made a small investment in the venture because of my growing interest in snow skiing. Eventually, Ski Haus became the leading year-round sport store in Cleveland, expanding to bikes and camping for the summer. It wasn't until I moved to Hawaii in 1977 that I sold my small interest in the Ski Haus.

In the summer of 1959 I received a call from another high school friend, Dale. He was a great salesperson and a habitual gambler. Although he almost always won at poker, he lost one of his houses trying to perfect a horse race system. His wife said she would divorce him if he continued trying to perfect the horse race system. This was the reason he reconnected. He asked me to buy six months of old copies of a daily newspaper called the *Daily Racing Form*. He used these instead of betting at the racetrack. Then two more times he asked for a six-month supply.

When he felt the system was ready, he gave me a copy of his work. I agreed to go to Tropical Race Track in Florida for one month and work his system (risking a maximum of $1,000). I rented a motel room for one month. This turned out to be great fun. The weather was wonderful, surroundings beautiful, and interesting crowds to watch. I arrived about eleven a.m. each day, bought a bowl of clam chowder (a standard with the crowd), and studied the Daily Racing Form. His system was very selective to the point where I only had one or two bets to place each day.

Yes, this could have been an ongoing business. At the end of the thirty days, I had made a very good profit; the system had worked. I returned to Cleveland since I wanted more to look forward to than just betting on the horses.

"Take from every experience what it has to offer."
—Henry Miller, *Author*

"Success… seems to be connected with action. Successful men keep moving. They make mistakes, but they don't quit."
—**Conrad Hilton,** *Hotelier*

CHAPTER 5

STOCK BROKERAGE FIRM (SS & COMPANY)

It was 1960. I joined a youthful brokerage firm in Cleveland, Ohio. Most of the sales people were about my age, in their thirties. The drill was to dial ten to twenty prospects a day. What I hated about that was using the rotary dial phones of the time. Numbers one through three were okay. But numbers zero, nine, eight, and seven? After dialing you had to wait for the dial to return. It was so slow; it seemed like forever. What a difference when push button dialing arrived. I enjoyed cold calling… most of the time. The exceptions were when people were having a bad day. Fortunately they were in the minority.

In 1962 I received a letter from the IRS and a phone call from an agent. I disputed his claim and requested a conference with his superior. During the past five years I had attended the IRS free year-end training for tax preparers, accountants, and CPAs. Actually, anyone could attend this all-day review of tax law changes. One of the new laws I learned of had to do with a change in how some stock tax losses could be utilized. I explained this new law to the IRS superior. He had never heard of it and refused to remove their complaint. Next I requested a meeting with the IRS district director. He also had not heard of the change and would do nothing. So, I appealed to the IRS tax court. They acknowledged my argument and dropped their claim. It was amazing to me that I had to teach the entire Cleveland IRS staff the new law. Don't give up when you feel you are correct. Later in my business career I also won my next three audits.

Some days were busier than others. On quieter days, I took the opportunity to learn other areas of the business. The firm had a one-man municipal (muny) bond department run by Mark. On those quieter days, I would sit in Mark's office, listen, and ask questions about muny bonds. After a few months of my digesting the muny bond operation, Mark got upset about something regarding his communication with Mr. D, the president of the firm, and lost his patience. He picked up the phone and called him. Mr. D was on the eleventh hole at his country club playing golf. Mark firmly demanded that the operator call him to the phone right away. After a slightly heated repartee there was a period of silence where Mark was just listening, listening, and listening. Mark then set the phone in its cradle. I asked, "What was that about?" He said, "I just got fired."

On keeping cool: "People who fly into a rage always make a bad landing."
—Will Rogers, *Humorist*

The next morning the president called me into his office. "Jack, do you know enough about muny bonds to run the department?" "Yes, I do," I said with a positive attitude. I became the manager of the muny bond department with a small salary. And, I could still sell stocks to my current clients and receive those commissions—just no more prospecting.

Part of the new position required me to fly from Cleveland to New York once a month to meet with our correspondent brokerage firm. They were cordial and helpful in assisting me with the takeover of the bond department. My firm had about one million dollars of "white elephant" municipal bonds in inventory. I was able to dispose of them without a loss.

One year later, I tallied the financial gains and losses for the bond department. There was a profit of $15,000 (about $175,000 forty-five years later). This was the first profit for this department in its fifteen-year existence.

The following week, upon returning from lunch, Mr. D called me into his office. He introduced me to the manager of the municipal bond department. I thought to myself, *What am I hearing. I was manager when I went to lunch. I return from lunch and I am not?* Some guy, Manny, walked into *my* firm during my lunch hour and sold the president what a GREAT muny bond manager he is. The president said I could sit in the muny office and listen and "learn" while still selling stocks—without the salary.

Yes, that was an unexpected punch in the gut. But I knew I would be further ahead by thinking the situation through, being patient, and planning my next move with a calm mind. Nothing would have been gained by exploding—as you will see after this storm passes.

Reward 5

In 1963 I flew to Vienna, Austria, to ski in Kitzbuhel for a week and meet a friend in Innsbruck for more skiing.

The flight was very long and tiring. I slept a day and a half before heading to the first ski area. A rental Volkswagen was my transportation from city to city. The German language competency that I developed when in the service continued to improve since I was using it every day. What a treat to enjoy the long ski runs that were challenging enough for an average skier. The weather was ideal.

It wasn't until I became president of the Cleveland Ski Club (two years later) that I started skiing at Vail. It was there, thanks to Bruno Sartoux, that I developed my skiing to where I could ski parallel, powder, and moguls. Bruno grew up in France and practiced with Jean Claude Killy, the French Winter Olympic Gold Medal winner in the 1968 Grenoble Winter Games. Killy won gold in the men's giant slalom, slalom, and downhill competitions. During the 1966–1967 season, Killy won twelve of the eighteen World Cup races.

Bruno became so popular as an instructor at Vail that in 1968 one man booked him for the entire winter season. It must have cost that man more than $30,000. I didn't get a ski lesson that year from Bruno.

"From quiet reflection will come even more effective action."
—Peter Drucker, *Management Expert*

CHAPTER 6

LEAR JET CORPORATION

Without saying a word to anyone, I planned to leave the brokerage firm. I decided to locate a leading executive placement organization. The one I selected was well known with nationwide offices. My capabilities and education qualified me to become assistant to the president of one of the top 500 corporations in the United States.

After creating the required four-page resume, I began mailing it to the first 200 of the top 500 firms. I received an offer from Bill Lear (1902–1978) of Lear Jet Corporation. My interview was in Wichita, Kansas. I found Bill to be a prince of a person and looked forward to working with him. Mr. Lear hired me soon thereafter.

I inquired about his eight-track stereo, and wondered where I could get one for my car. In that moment, Bill called the eight-track plant in Michigan. After the call, he told me to drive to the Detroit plant. They would be expecting me and would install the stereo while I waited. In addition to installing the stereo, I was also supplied with special factory-recorded tapes. On the return to Cleveland, the stereo sounded as though I were in a concert hall with the four surround sound speakers gently stimulating my eardrums.

Later, in Wichita, Mr. Lear and I are still discussing my stock options. A call came to me from the president of the brokerage firm I had just left. Mr. D wanted me back. He offered me titles of secretary, treasurer, and director of the firm; increased salary; stock options; and manager of the cashiering department. I said, "Thank you; I will call you later." Bill asked, "What was that about?"

After sharing this with Bill, he saw this as a great offer and suggested I accept. I indicated how much I wanted to work for him, but Bill felt I should not pass this up; we could continue to be close friends. And so it was.

I would become part owner of the Cleveland brokerage firm. Because of the potential growth I saw for Lear Jet Corporation, I wrote a report (which was published) recommending it as a wise investment. In appreciation, Mr. Lear invited me to attend the private board of directors' meetings* held prior to the stockholder meetings. Board meeting are generally closed to the public. (* see glossary)

Another time, when I called Bill from Las Vegas just to say hello, he suggested I get on a plane and fly to visit him at his home in Palm Springs and stay overnight. One of Bill's pilots met me at the airport. As we are driving to Mr. Lear's home, we are going through some beautiful neighborhoods. I notice a black four-door Cadillac backing into the street. I look at the driver and recognize Ike Eisenhower with Mamie seated next to him. Another exciting but fleeting and special moment.

When I arrived at Bill's home, he apologized that there would be another guest: the president of Flying Tiger Airlines. Of course I didn't mind. Upon awaking the next morning, I smelled bacon frying. In the kitchen was Bill cooking breakfast (with eggs, toast, coffee, etc.) for the three of us. After breakfast, Bill asked where I would be going next. I told him that I was going to Cleveland. "Fine," he said, "we'll take my jet to Wichita for a short stop, then on to New York with a stop in Cleveland to drop you off." At the time I thought, *Is this really happening?* Perhaps I had better pinch myself.

On another visit to Wichita, Bill and his copilot invited me to experience their testing new spoilers. We flew to 41,000 feet. Just three of us were in the plane. The copilot called back to me to be sure I was belted in. "We're going to test the spoilers." The plane dropped like a rock for about 9,000 feet. That was some feeling. Their comment: "Well, they worked as planned."

Later in life, Mr. Lear was experimenting with hydrogen-powered engines for busses and trucks. Earlier in life, with only an eighth-grade education, he earned over 150 patents for groundbreaking electronic devices in three industries. The patents included the first practical automobile radio, the airplane radio-compass, and the autopilot.

During Bill's first marriage, he had two children. His daughter's name was Shanda. Do you see his sense of humor there?

On Foresight: "The future belongs to those who see possibilities before they become obvious."
—**John Sculley,** *Businessman*

Chapter 7

Rejoining the Brokerage Firm

Upon my return, I learned that Manny, who replaced me as the muny bond department manager about a year before, was fired after three or four months on the job. He cost the firm over $50,000 (in 1965). The firm was left with more "white elephant" inventory as a result of bad buying decisions.

After six months back at the brokerage firm, and managing the cashiering department, Mr. D called me into his office. One of the girls in my ten-person department was complaining that Janet kept coming in around nine-thirty a.m. instead of eight. Janet was the best of all the people in the cashiering department— always completing twice as much as the others in half the time. She came in late because she helped her boyfriend close his bar around two a.m. And, in these years, no one had considered alternate time schedules in the office, e.g. eight to four for some, nine to five for others. Mr. D "ordered" me to fire her. He could not understand alternate schedules. That was my first and my most difficult firing.

Approximately ten months later, the sales staff has increased from fourteen to about twenty-six. This meant that the buy transactions, sales transactions, checks in, and checks out almost doubled. I told the president that I needed more employees. His said, "You don't need more employees; the computer does all the work," according to the Midwest Stock Exchange salesman who sold him the computer. And, he totally believed this.

Our "computer" was an IBM punch card processing machine—nothing like computers in the twenty-first century. We created one card for each purchase, sale, payment, and cash out, then processed them separately. Unfortunately, we were getting more and more behind.

31

A few months later, with the sales staff at thirty, I asked for more employees. The president's response was, "I'll have the MWSE computer salesman, Jerry, come in to appraise the situation."

When Jerry arrived from Chicago, we had a chance to meet privately for a few moments. He told me that he understood the situation, and that he would represent my best interests. Ha! That didn't happen. After Jerry's meeting with the president, I was called into his office and "introduced" to the new manager of the cashiering department. This seemed like a repeat of my replacement as manager of the municipal bond department. Per Mr. D, I get to keep all my titles but give up the 60 percent balance of my stock options, as well as my salary. I'm now a stock salesman again working on commission. Immediately the cashiering department hired seven more employees. *Hmmmm?* I thought. And I was refused three or four.

Once again I keep my cool, left Mr. D's office, and pondered what my next step would be. It was 1968 and I was also aware that the firm was about to be involved in a "hot" stock offering. The firm had 200,000 pre-offering shares at a cost of one dollar each, and the stock would come public at fifteen dollars. That would increase the firm's net worth by about $3 million—as well as the value of my $13,000 of stock options to over $100,000.

About three months later, Mr. D had to fire Jerry. He was too slick for his own good. In order to make the department look current, he put all the accounts receivable into one computer account. In actuality, it became almost impossible to locate detail. The cost to the firm was over $100,000. It took two CPA firms six months to rearrange all of our accounts. Unfortunately, these events represented Mr. D's inability to make good decisions. At the time there were about twenty people in the cashiering department.

As I was still secretary, treasurer, and director, Mr. D called me into his office to meet with the firm's attorney. The attorney explained that the firm's stock repurchase agreement was updated, and I had to get every stockholder to sign the new document. At that time there were about thirty-five stockholders.

Thanks to my legal background, it was obvious what was being done. The original repurchase agreement was a simple and fair one-page document. This new agreement was three pages, complicated, and unfair. It gave the firm six months to "decide" if they wanted to buy a person's stock and the right to decide how much and in what form a stockholder would be paid. I had to get every stockholder's signature. When asked if I had signed mine yet, I said (honestly), "Not yet, but we all have to sign it." After getting all the signatures, I returned all the documents to the attorney.

Time passes. The underwriting was successful and the $15 stock underwriting rose to $50. In late 1969 I was fed up with the incompetence of the president. Plus my stock in the firm was worth at least $250,000.

I ask the president for a meeting in his office. I resigned and indicated that my stock was worth about $250,000. "Oh," he said, "remember that new stock repurchase agreement? We have decided to give you about $90,000 from investments in our inventory that we don't want anymore."

Then came my moment of retribution. "But, I did not sign that agreement." The executive vice president and the president's jaws drop. Mr. D immediately phoned the attorney and called him into the meeting in a loud commanding voice. "Now," he said to the attorney. The first thing the attorney said to me after arriving to the meeting was, "Why didn't you tell me you didn't sign the agreement?" "Wasn't it your responsibility to check each agreement?" I asked.

"Meeting is adjourned," said the president gruffly, and the three left the room.

I hired a major law firm in Cleveland and we settled for $190,000 cash. My patience was rewarded, and I was the only stockholder to be paid for his shares. I was lucky to have decided to leave the firm when I did.

Six months later the firm filed for bankruptcy. The Stirling-Homex $15 underwriting went from $50 to 50 cents in one day when some hidden/undisclosed facts surfaced. And, SS & Company's net worth virtually evaporated.

The business of Stirling-Homex was the complete construction of modular housing on one assembly line. Since every city has different zoning laws, the low-cost housing modular homes could not just be bolted to a foundation. Requests for zoning changes had to be filed in each city, which delayed the genuine closing and payment for the sales. During this time, construction continued to increase—along with the purported sales. And, published news of this increasing construction caused the stock to climb. But sales were made to and through a separate, secret, but associated "distribution company." As a result, these completed homes were stacked like dominos on hundreds of acres of farmland while awaiting delivery. Not only did the stock became worthless, Merrill Lynch, who raised $65 million for Stirling-Homex, had to return all those funds due to their failure to disclose these hidden facts. The CPAs for Stirling-Homex were also heavily fined for this lack of disclosure.

"I'm a great believer in luck, and I find the harder I work the more I have of it."
—**Thomas Jefferson,** *Third U. S. President*

On Achievement: "Whatever course you have chosen for yourself, it will not be a chore but an adventure if you bring to it a sense of the glory of striving, if your sights are set far above the merely secure and mediocre."
—**David Sarnoff,** *Broadcast Pioneer*

"Learn from the mistakes of others. You can never live long enough to make them all yourself."
—**Groucho Marx,** *Comedian*

"Only those who dare to fall greatly can ever achieve greatly."
—**Robert Kennedy,** *Former U. S. Attorney General*

Chapter 8

Gross Tal Ski Resort,

Western New York State

While in the military, I had an opportunity to take my first ski lesson in Berchtesgarten, Germany. Seven years later while in Cleveland, I served as treasurer of the Cleveland Ski Club. The following year I was elected president. During that time I was invited to join a group of eight who planned to purchase Gross Tal. As a corporation, this group of eight decided to install snowmaking equipment. Gross Tal was the first ski area in Western New York State to have snowmaking capabilities. For me, this was a casual investment.

Once the snowmaking equipment was up and running, we were swamped with skiers. Skiers loved the area and we investors loved the crowds.

One Sunday, halfway into the winter season, I was in line to get on the two-seat ski lift along with my date, Kathy, the "queen" of the Cleveland Ski Club. We were about six couples away from boarding the lift. Suddenly my attention was frozen on the chair lift; it seemed to be moving backward. It *was* moving backward, and picking up speed. Every seat was occupied. I was informed later that the lift attained a speed of 35 miles per hour, in reverse, before it became weight balanced and stopped.

The fright was so overwhelming that some people jumped out of their chairs, even though they were high up. It was gut wrenching to see those people drop. Fortunately, on this day, most of the ski patrol members from this area were at our resort for training. The ski patrol was challenged for all of their abilities and did a remarkable job. Those who jumped suffered injuries. The others were lowered to the ground. One small boy was thrown out of the chair in the wheel-house. People yelled at him repeatedly to lay flat. But he kept trying to get up and died from his injuries.

How did this happen? Our facilities had been checked by the State of New York months earlier and were certified for the season. Later, after detailed research, the manufacturer, supplier, and installer of the ski lift had installed the wrong length of steel brake pins in the braking mechanism. The pins were too long, and they snapped from the weight of the fully occupied lift.

Even though the lift was eventually repaired, trust was lost. Skiers no longer wanted to return to Gross Tal that season or the following season. Our investment was lost, and we transferred our interest to a new owner.

Regarding liability, since the State of New York had inspected the ski area's facilities and gave it their stamp of approval, we had done all we could do. The company in Switzerland was liable. But to sue someone in another country was determined not to be cost effective for us or the State of New York. Generally speaking, as a stockholder in a corporation, we were exempted from personal liability.

Reward 6

After the business venture discussed in chapter eight, I was invited by my Officers' Club employee/friend Werner Henkelmann to meet him in the Canary Islands. He had just bought a new one-bedroom condo on Tenerife. I booked a two-week Iberia Airline flight/tour from New York City, leaving about a week before New Year's 1970. After stops in Madrid and Barcelona, I got off the plane in Las Palmas de Gran Canaria (the largest of the islands). From there I got a flight to Tenerife Island (city of Santa Cruz). Werner was at the airport with his VW van that he had previously shipped from Germany. We drove from the northern half of the island to his condo in the southern half. The Islands (seven in total) were under Spanish control. This became my paradise until I later visited Hawaii. They are so alike: both with seven islands and similar weather.

Werner's condo was at the ocean. We only had electricity during the day while the workers had the generators running. The entire project was only about one-third finished when I was there. In the evening we used candles. In order to cook, we went shopping the next day for a small gas burner. Then we could enjoy dinner in the condo. For lunch, we would drive to one of the several nearby towns for a *paella*. The *paella* is a Valencian rice dish from the eastern coast of Spain. Since almost every chef has his or her own version of a *paella*, Werner and I ordered a different one each day. As is true with fun vacations, time passes too quickly.

My tour continued on to Madeira Island, which was under Portuguese control. I arrived in Funchal, and took a taxi to the hotel where the tour group was staying. The tour director said there were no more vacancies at the hotel, and that he would make calls to get me a hotel room. I must have had a lucky star following me around; he found me a room at Reid's Palace Hotel. This hotel had over 100 years of history, and Sir Winston Churchill used to be a frequent guest. Considered to be among the world's finest hotels, Reid's has become famous for its discreet service and impeccable tradition. As my taxi arrived at the hotel, my attention shifted to the twenty-foot–high cement retaining wall across from the hotel. It was totally covered with purple flowers—my first introduction to the bougainvillea plant.

The hotel is situated in its own ten acres of lush, subtropical gardens sprawling down a majestic cliff and overlooking the bay and the lively city of Funchal. After checking in to my room, I went to the dining room for lunch. Maybe I was dressed to casually, but the *maître d'hotel* soon asked me, "Are you staying in the hotel?" After saying I just checked in, I was treated superbly and asked for my last name. That evening, when I arrived for dinner the greeting was, "Good evening Mr. Terry. Our special this evening is leg of lamb." The *maître d'* even remembered my name. I did order the leg of lamb for dinner. Little did I expect they would roll out a cart with the entire leg and ask me which portion I would like.

I had breakfast served to me on one of the terraces, with wicker tables and chairs and views of the Atlantic Ocean and Port Funchal below.

Then it was off to Lisbon for our last stop. A day later I was on my way back to New York City.

Reward 7

During the summer of 1970, a travel agent friend was telling me about a two-week trip to Asia that he was selling to the Ohio Medical Association. It was one week in Japan, with hotel and breakfasts, and one week in Hong Kong with hotel and breakfasts, and round-trip airfare, for just $750. "How can I get on this trip?" I asked. "Well," he said, "I can set up your reservation as Dr. Terry. The trip would also include a Japanese Bullet Train ride to Osaka to attend "Expo Seventy." My check was in the travel agent's hand the next day.

I began recalling my undergrad college days and, specifically, a classmate from Bangkok, Thailand. The university didn't have any record of his home address since he attended only two years at Miami University. Having no idea of the size of Bangkok, I wrote a letter to Wishai Leamrong, Bangkok, Thailand, with no address or zip code. Later I learned it was a city of several million people. But he got my letter. A female postal employee happened to see my letter, took it home to her son (who worked for Wishai), and he delivered it the next day. I must also have an Asian guardian angel! Wishai was in charge of general administration for the Bank of Thailand (a very prestigious position). Wishai answered me and said he would meet me at whatever hotel I checked in to.

I started in Tokyo. Tokyo was a delightful, clean city, with everything running on time (trains, busses, etc.) If a tourist was not on a prepaid tour, everything could be very expensive. I never learned Japanese, but many did speak English. The Bullet Train ride was thrilling, topping out at over 100 miles per hour. "Expo '70" was like an enormous amusement park. If you didn't get in the park before noon, you had to return the next day (the gates closed after the first "half-million" people entered each day). The Japanese seem to love "events."

At my college reunion in 2012, my waitress at lunch looked Japanese. I started a conversation about Japan and asked if she was born there. After her "yes" answer, I mentioned that I was there for Expo '70. Her unexpected response was that she was a model at that expo. Once more I thought how small the world has become.

After the flight to Hong Kong, we checked in to the Mandarin Oriental—another elegant experience. It has been the center of Hong Kong's social and business scene since 1963. About a month earlier I took a cooking class from a Cordon Bleu chef in Cleveland, and knew a little about a crepe (a very thin pancake, usually made from wheat flour) and a soufflé (a puffed-up cake made with egg yolks and beaten egg whites). One evening I noticed on the menu a desert special: a soufflé within a crepe. This was something else new to me, so I had to order it. The soufflé was lemon flavored within the crepe covered with a raspberry wine sauce. As we sometimes say, it was "to die for." What a treat! I devoured it slowly so as to lengthen the gastronomical pleasure.

Of course this hotel had a Chinese restaurant. But it was different. There were linen tablecloths and the wait staff were all in tuxedos. It was here that I first learned to use chopsticks.

It was time for my midweek, three-day side trip to Bangkok. I booked a room at the new Dusit Thani Hotel. The flight to Bangkok was on a small twin-engine propeller plane. On the way we flew over a fairly large river. Upon inquiry I was told it was the Mekong River in Vietnam. Oops, I didn't want to hear that. The Vietnam War was still waging. Soon we were landing in Bangkok and I took a taxi to the hotel. Wishai picked me up and drove to his office for one quick bit of business. I followed him. Every employee at the bank backed against the wall and saluted as he went by. How different are some country conventions. Wishai's English was perfect, as was his wife's, who worked for the American Embassy. I was treated like a dignitary. I was even taken on an early morning canal trip through the farmers' market, a floating market on long, narrow riverboats like we were on. Wishai had not done this before even though he grew up there. He also showed me his homes. There were three of them on two acres about ten minutes from downtown Bangkok with maids in each house.

Then I returned to Hong Kong. Upon boarding the plane, it taxied to the runway. We sat for about ten minutes, and then it taxied back. Fifteen minutes later we taxied to the runway, and after about fifteen minutes we taxied back again. Fifteen minutes later we finally took off and soon were back in Hong Kong. At baggage claim, there was a commanding announcement: "Pick up your baggage and stand by it until further notice." One bag remained unclaimed. The newspaper headlines the next morning explained: $100,000 American Dollars were left unclaimed at the terminal the night before. A drug ring courier avoided capture.

CHAPTER 9

A RESTAURANT IN STEAMBOAT SPRINGS

Alongtime friend, Larry Torian, suggested we open a restaurant in Steamboat Springs, Colorado. Larry was a renowned portrait artist as well as an experienced restaurateur.

Another friend, Jess, an owner and operator of a nationally known cosmetic company, was the third owner. Jess and I would just be investors and Larry would move from Cleveland to operate the restaurant. Larry's parents had several restaurants on the west side of Cleveland. Each would invest $20,000 into a corporation and own one-third of the restaurant. This was another one of my casual investments. After we opened, I would fly to Steamboat one week each month to ski and eat.

Upon arriving in Steamboat, Larry started looking for a location. Each of us agreed that our menu should offer American-style food along with some Southwestern choices. We formed a limited liability corporation (LLC). Larry arranged for the necessary permits and a liquor license. A good chef was also located (unfortunately, he loved to ski—not the best combination).

The "ideal" location turned out to be the oldest home in the valley, but at the base of a major ski slope. The small porch was enlarged to become an art gallery. Some interior walls were removed to create a sizeable dining room and bar/lounge. Larry painted the exterior of the house purple, and named the restaurant Torian's Plum. After its completion we were ready for the ski season.

Even though Steamboat was a new resort, it had a great variety of slopes. Some skiers referred to it as a small version of Vail. But, being new, the owners/developers had not yet developed summer attractions.

Our restaurant did very well our first winter. *Town & Country* magazine named Torian's Plum as having the best food among thirty-three restaurants in Steamboat. Among our first year customers were Ethyl Kennedy and Robert Redford.

Our first summer was not only lacking the amount of customers we experienced during the winter, but many of our costs remained. We did not want to lose our chef, so we continued his salary throughout the year. This reduced our winter profits to the extent we decided not to issue any dividends. Fortunately the developers rapidly expanded the summer attractions so we could anticipate a better summer the next year.

Our second winter (1972–1973) started with a healthy increase in business. Halfway through this second winter, our ski-loving chef broke his leg on the slopes. What to do now? We were fully booked for dinner that evening. Well, Larry proved his value based on his experience. He kept the kitchen operating until the chef could get around with his cast.

With a very good second winter season behind us, we anticipated some improvements during our second summer. The developers had added golf courses, tennis courts, and hiking programs to attract a summer trade. Summer reservations were very encouraging.

Then there was the mid-1970s gasoline shortage. Denver gas stations had limited supplies and long lines. The drive to Steamboat from Denver took several hours. The potential summer guests worried they might get stranded in Steamboat. So, the anticipated summer season didn't happen.

To say the least, Larry, Jess, and I were quite upset. After numerous meetings, we decided to sell the restaurant. Our asking price was the same as our original investment (since we had not yet been able to extend our property lease beyond the first three years). With Jess and I in Cleveland, Larry was charged with handling the sale.

There was an interested buyer who was willing to pay $60,000. In the meantime, Larry continued talking to the landlord regarding a lease extension. Thinking he was close to getting a five-year extension, Larry raised the asking price to $90,000 without discussing the change with his partners. This caused the potential buyer to walk away.

Larry knew he had lost the sale and went into a heavy depression, which required him to spend several months in a hospital. Jess and I decided to close the restaurant and walk away. We could apply the loss against other income. The memories were great, but the investment wasn't.

"I am not discouraged, because every wrong attempt discarded is another step forward."
—**Thomas Edison,** *Inventor*

"The only people who have the easy answers are the people who don't have the responsibility."
—**Clarence Thomas,** *U. S. Supreme Court Justice*

"Far better is it to dare mighty things, to win glorious triumphs, even though checkered by failure than to rank with those poor spirits who neither enjoy much nor suffer much, because they live in a gray twilight that knows not victory nor defeat."
—**Theodore Roosevelt,** *Twenty-sixth U. S. President*

CHAPTER 10

COMMODITY MUTUAL FUNDS

After leaving SS & Company I met a commodity trading specialist named Jim. My curiosity about commodity trading led to a friendship with him. I learned that this area of the securities business traded corn, wheat, soybeans, gold, oil, and natural gas, among other things. It appears to be the quickest way to lose money if you don't know what you are doing.

I tested Jim by having him make a cattle trade. Within a week, I cleared about $1,500.

Jim had a dream of creating a commodity mutual fund. In doing so, this would have been a first for the industry. To simplify the formation, I suggested a limited partnership whereby there would be ten units. I would sell eight of the units for $5,000 each and Jim and I would each receive one unit for our efforts, and we would be the general partner. Our own cash investment was minimal—less than $1,000. This buisness was actually "funded" with Jim's expertise and my sales efforts.

Once I completed the legal work, and brought in eight investors, "Commodity Fund Alpha" was ready to trade with $40,000. After the first month, the profit was about 20 percent ($8,000). Wow, that was exciting, to say the least.

One of my friends was the editor of a local weekly newspaper. He agreed to list our results each week. This transparency added value and public interest in our program.

At the end of the second month, our "Alpha" fund had a value of $60,000—a

50 percent gain. At that point, Jim and I decided to create a second fund. We named it "Commodity Fund Beta." Again, eight of the ten units each sold for $5,000.

After six months, the "Alpha" fund had a net worth of over $200,000. We were now invested in a "short" of twenty contracts of silver. Jim was planning on taking profits in another day or two. Unfortunately that never happened.

A war between Egypt and Israel started. In time of war, precious metals (like silver and gold) rise quickly in value as a security versus other monies or property. Each day thereafter, silver was "up-limit" for a week or so on each day's opening trade. The "up-limit" rule limited the amount a commodity could rise or fall in price in one day. If that happened on the opening trade of the day, then there would be no more trades for the day. This meant that you could not liquidate your position until this "limit rule" was no longer in effect. In our situation, we could not buy out of our "short" position and take our profits. We could only watch our "Alpha" fund drop in value each "up-limit" day.

When the market finally stabilized, the value of "Alpha" was almost back to where we started. I reviewed our situation with each investor. The group decision was to liquidate. The investors got their money back.

"You may be disappointed if you fail, but you are doomed if you don't try."
—Beverly Sills, *Singer*

"All business proceeds on beliefs, or judgments of probabilities, and not on certainties."
—William Hewlett, *Hewlett-Packard Co-founder*

Critique

In the securities business, you are not trading the market, you are trading the human behavior of other people. Confidence-building factors become everything. Get your brain in sync with market uncertainties. Confidence is a feeling. Feelings and emotions supersede intellect.
—Denise Shull, *Market Maker/Investor/Trainer*

CHAPTER 11

STRIP MALL SHOPPING CENTER

I attended several business groups from time to time. At one of these meetings I met Dr. Mark O'Keefe, an orthodontist. As our friendship developed, he invited me to join him in purchasing a strip mall consisting of over 100,000 square feet of leasable space along with two freestanding buildings.

This mall, except for one small space, was fully leased and located in a popular neighborhood. The mall needed some exterior upgrading and the replacement of a couple air-conditioning units. It was Mark's belief that lease rents could easily be increased once these improvements were completed, My investment was to be $30,000 for a 30-percent ownership in the corporation holding title. My attorney met with his attorney to execute the necessary papers.

Mark owned many other rental properties. Consequently, I was able to learn much about operating and managing commercial real estate. He had me walk the roof of this strip mall to check its overall condition. I learned that future maintenance could be very high if the roof wasn't properly and timely maintained. We also talked to several of the tenants, including the freestanding unit operators, to see if they had any needs that were not being taken care of.

With this knowledge, we could help them to increase their business and likewise grow our revenue. The benefit to us was that some of the tenants paid rent based on a percentage of their gross sales.

After the first year, all the improvements that Mark had planned were completed. This did result in the overall sales for the mall to increase, along with our lease income.

About this time, I was presented with another investment opportunity and needed additional funds. Mark was understanding and agreed to buy back my 30-percent ownership for $33,000 (a 10-percent profit). In addition, I gained knowledge in an industry that to me had previously been foreign.

"There's an old Wayne Gretzky quote that I love, 'I skate to where the puck is going to be, not where it has been.' And we've always tried to do that at Apple, since the very, very beginning. And we always will."
—**Steve Jobs,** *(1955–2011) Apple Co-founder*

On Vision: "Part of the issue of achievement is to be able to set realistic goals, but that's one of the hardest things to do because you don't always know exactly where you're going, and you shouldn't."
—**George Lucas,** *Filmmaker*

CHAPTER 12

ARTHUR TREACHER'S FISH & CHIPS

With the substantial payoff from the brokerage firm in the bank, I was looking for an investment that would provide a regular income. Recalling that a law school classmate had developed a very successful chain of seven fish and chip restaurants in Ohio, I arranged to meet with him. Gus's locations had been operating profitably for about ten years.

Timing was right. Gus was planning to open another chain of Arthur Treacher's Fish & Chip restaurants, this time in Connecticut. A one-quarter ownership was still available for $50,000. I accepted and said to Gus, "This is the largest check I have ever written; take good care of it." In return I received shares of stock representing 25 percent of the corporation.

Several months later, our first Arthur Treacher's restaurant was ready to open in Hartford. I brought my mother to enjoy the gala affair. The real Arthur Treacher was there, and it was quite a thrill for my mother to meet him.

Mr. Treacher (1894–1975) was an English actor born in Brighton, England. He was a veteran of World War I and established a stage career in 1928. He was well known for portraying the perfect valet (butler) with a height of six-feet-four-inches. He danced side by side in four movies with tiny Shirley Temple. In addition he was Merv Griffin's announcer and sidekick on the *Merv Griffin Show*. During this period of popularity, he capitalized on his name recognition and image for Arthur Treacher's Fish & Chips (which grew to almost 900 outlets).

With the first location doing very well, Gus met with the owners to get approval to expand. With this goal approved, Gus leased three locations that had sold hamburgers. The benefit was that the buildings were ideally located with plenty of drive-in parking. Also, the inside changes were much less than if we had constructed a new building on a vacant lot (as was done with the first location).

Another location became available that was adjacent to the main event center in downtown Hartford. That location and the first location were greatly successful. The second, third, and forth locations were closed within one year. The problem was that TV advertising wasn't as effective in Hartford as in Ohio. When the ads ran in Ohio, business always rebounded. This was not so in Hartford. After analyzing the situation, it seemed there were already too many other seafood restaurants.

In 1980, after about seven years of being unable to grow in Hartford as Gus did in Ohio, he suggested selling. All investors agreed, and our original investment was returned.

On a positive note, I had invested with an honest and capable partner.

On Risk: "If you want to achieve a high goal, you're going to have to take some chances."
—Alberto Salazar, *Marathon Runner*

> "As long as you're going to be thinking anyway, think big."
> —**Donald Trump,** *Real Estate Magnate*

CHAPTER 13

THE BOEING 707 TRAVEL CLUB

After leaving the SS & Company brokerage firm, I joined another broker-age firm as a vice president for about two years. This allowed me to keep in touch with my favorite clients. Also, I developed several new male friends who were my age and looking into investment ideas. The most promising was the creation of a travel club, which would operate out of Cleveland, Ohio. This would require the purchase of a Boeing 707 passenger jet that carried 176 passengers. Our operating license would come from the U. S. Federal Aviation Administration (FAA).

The FAA supervised "safety" for all airlines. Within the United States there were six other travel clubs operating out of different cities, with the largest club in Indianapolis (with three jets).

Two corporations were formed. Corporation A would own the jet and be a profit center. Corporation B was to be the non-profit travel club, renting the plane from Corporation A. A lease-purchase agreement would be executed with Pan Am World Airways, requiring a monthly payment of around $25,000. This lease in-cluded full maintenance anywhere in the world.

The plane cost us $1,050,000, with a deposit of $100,000 split equally be-tween the four owners (Regis, Tony, George, and me).

We took delivery and executed the agreements in Freeport, Bahamas, which saved us about $60,000 in sales taxes. The plane had been in regular passenger service for about ten years.

All four of us arrived in Freeport to sign the agreements of lease purchase. A Pan Am ferry crew flew the plane to Freeport to cover the legal technicalities of taking delivery outside the United States. At the same time we approved the refurbishing of the inside and the special painting of the outside. Along the length of the body was the travel club's name: Aeronauts International Travel Club. On the tail was our logo—a rendering of the world.

My partners were married and remained in Freeport for a short vacation. I returned to Miami with the ferry crew. What a memory: just me and the pilots on "my" jet flying to Miami. I was in and out of the cockpit and back and forth in the plane like a kid with a new toy.

Then came the challenges of operating the club. First, we had to hire a cockpit crew. In those days the plane was required to have a pilot, copilot, engineer, and navigator. Next we had to hire several crews of stewardesses (as they were called then), with four ladies in each crew (one for each fifty seats or fraction thereof).

Once the basic team was formed, they had to be approved as to their competency by the FAA. This meant an emergency evacuation drill for the stewardesses. With the plane on the ground in Miami, the stewardesses had to evacuate 176 "passengers" and cockpit crew within ninety seconds while supervised by the FAA team.

In order to fill the plane, we advertised in the local papers inviting the public to take a seat and experience an evacuation, in return for a monetary fee. All the owners also took a seat and got to slide down an evacuation chute. Our stewardesses did a very commendable job. They passed the test on the first try.

Next the pilots had to take to the air with the FAA onboard and fly a pattern and return to the airport. Our pilot crew had flown on several airlines all over the world and was very experienced. But, when they returned to land, the landing gear would not drop into position hydraulically. They had to hand-crank the wheels into place. Not good. It was our first failure.

The Pan Am maintenance team replaced the hydraulic motor. With their thumbs up, we scheduled another test flight. It was another failure. We failed five more times after that.

Our inaugural flight, sold out with a waiting list of twenty, was now only a week away. Our planned schedule was from Cleveland to Honolulu on Monday and return on Tuesday with the group from the week before.

What now? We had to do this flight or lose credibility. Chartering another plane was our only answer. We had lost money on that flight, but the passengers had their promised vacation. Our advertised price was $265 for a round-trip ticket to Honolulu, with transfers and one week's hotel room stay in Waikiki.

In the meantime we are looking for our own maintenance person. Several applied, but none would be our first choice.

On one of my trips to Miami, I was introduced to a man who was in charge of maintaining seven C-130 military aircraft in the Pacific. He was a down-to-earth and sincere person, married with two children and a qualifying background record. What a stroke of good fortune at a critical point in our ability to continue operating. "Jerry" met and was approved by all officers.

Every time the hydraulic system failed to lower the wheels, Pan Am had to replace the hydraulic motor at a cost of $1,800 each.

Jerry went up on the next flight to experience what was happening. That was failure number eight.

Where Pan Am's maintenance people couldn't solve the problem, Jerry did. He pointed out that the neoprene tubing was like a human artery leading to a heart attack—"plaque" buildup.

The same was true with our tubing. Oil slowly built up, reducing the size of the tube to the point that it created back pressure on the hydraulic system. The cost to repair it was only a $10 piece of new neoprene tubing. Soon thereafter, Pan Am had all older Boeing 707s around the world replace the tubing on a programed time schedule.

Now we were approved (attempt number nine) to fly passengers. After that first approved flight, all was proceeding on schedule. Except, we hadn't made a lease payment because there had been no income due to the delays. At that time every flight to Honolulu had a waiting list of twenty people, and we started to experience profitability. We could see the light at the end of the tunnel.

Then a legal notice from Pan Am threatening to cancel our lease purchase agreement for non-payment over the last three months. My thinking was that this came from the leasing department, and the senior officers were not aware of our situation.

My associates became totally discouraged. I offered to go with Jerry to Pan Am's headquarters and meet with top management. I was sure they were not aware of what we had been through regarding the landing equipment failures. My associates expressed that I would be wasting my time. I went anyway.

Pan Am's top brass cordially greeted Jerry and me. After explaining our situation (which the top brass were not aware of), I presented what I felt was a fair arrangement. First, I asked them to totally excuse the three months of unpaid lease amounts. Second, I asked them to give us two more months free of lease payments. Third, I reiterated how Jerry solved a major failure that their own maintenance people could not locate. This eventually benefitted their entire airline fleet. The result was that the top brass totally agreed with my requests.

When Jerry and I returned to Cleveland, my partners did not believe what I had accomplished at first. When they finally accepted this new reality, we were full steam (or should I say jet power) ahead with our Monday flight to Honolulu, which returned on Tuesday.

With all flights having a waiting list of about twenty people, we set up an additional schedule between Wednesday and Sunday. These destinations varied each week between three resorts: Las Vegas, Acapulco, and the Bahamas. The Wednesday to Sunday crew would stay over with the passengers. This additional schedule also required a second cockpit crew and more stewardesses. Soon we had our own stewardess flight training school. We even trained stewardesses for other travel and charter clubs.

During one summer month, we varied our weekly schedule. We flew to Brussels, Belgium, one week and the next week to Yugoslavia. The next two weeks repeated this schedule, after which we returned to our Hawaii schedule.

Our first flight to Europe wasn't without incident. The Civil Aeronautics Board (CAB) didn't want us to fly to Europe. Why? The CAB represented and controlled the scheduled airlines within the United States and were jealous of our independence. As I mentioned before, we were licensed by the FAA, allowing us to independently follow FAA rules. In an attempt to exercise their "power" over us, the CAB pulled a dirty and dangerous action against Aeronauts International Travel Club.

You might wonder, "How was the CAB created?" At the end of World War II, the government wanted to control the growing airline business. The heads of the four major airlines at that time got wind of this government action. They went to the politicians planning this regulation and said, "We have been doing this and have the experience to understand what will work best for the industry." The government agreed and officially set up the CAB, granting them their own administrative court, their own administrative judge, and subpoena power. From that point forward, the CAB decided which airlines got certain routes and what rates should be charged passengers. Afterward, the CAB virtually answered to no one. In addition, they controlled "charter" flights but not travel clubs.

Getting back to the actions taken by the CAB. We asked why again, but they would not give us an answer, just repeating that they did not want us flying outside the United States.

Our first flight to Europe was airborne and beyond the halfway point (where there would not be enough fuel to return to the States). At that point, our flight captain received a call from the Brussels airport. "Your landing rights have been withdrawn!" This required our flight captain to contact other countries for landing permission. Fortunately, they received permission from Luxemburg. Also, arrangements had to be made to hire busses to take the passengers to Brussels.

For those citizens who are not yet aware of the complications and restraints that Big Government and self-endowed powerful politicians can inflict on citizens: be aware and fight back every chance you get. Perhaps two terms (eight years) should be the max for all elected officials, with no lifetime retirement benefits.

Jerry, our maintenance chief, was highly regarded by all for having solved the landing gear problem and for professionally validating my presentation to the Pan Am brass. Sadly, he left the world too soon. One day, on his way home to his wife and children, a drunk driver jumped the median strip of a four-lane highway and killed Jerry on impact. Borrowing from Charles Dickens, who commented on making a difference, Jerry was "lightening the burdens of others." This is how Jerry shall always be remembered.

After all the above, we continued to fly for almost a year, with waiting lists of about twenty on every flight.

Then there was another bombshell. An even bigger bombshell! We, along with the other six travel clubs, were subpoenaed to appear in Washington, D.C., one club at a time in the CAB court. The "charge" was "letting people on board who were not members." This was false since every passenger was checked to our member list as they were entering the plane. This CAB trial could be compared to a Kangaroo Court—false charges and a false judgment. All seven clubs were shut down. And the CAB told all airports in the country not to service us, including sale of gasoline.

Again, what next? If we could sell the plane, we could personally break even. Pan Am would not let us show the plane to our prospective buyers, suggesting that "we might fly away with it." Also, Pan Am knew that if we were not flying, we would not make the next lease payment. Then they could legally repossess the plane. That is what happened, and they sold the plane to one of our prospects.

All of these actions against us and the other six travel clubs ranged from unfair to illegal. The largest travel club in Indianapolis had the financial ability to sue the CAB on the behalf of all of us. After five years, in 1980, the case reached the U. S. Supreme Court. Their finding was that what was done to us was not only illegal, but criminally illegal.

Unfortunately, this was an empty win. The year before the airlines were deregulated by the government, and the CAB ceased to exist. This meant we had no one to collect from, even though we had a Supreme Court judgment.

On Perseverance: "Nobody grows old by merely living a number of years. People grow old by deserting their ideals."
—Douglas MacArthur, *General*

"The bigger the government, the more our innate freedoms are taken away. To restore our freedoms, big government must shrink."
—Jack Terry, *Entrepreneur*

Reward 7 ½

During the summers from 1971 to 1976 I vacationed in Canada two or three weekends each month. I bought a small camper to save the costs of reserving a room in a nearby motel. The camper was parked within a 100-acre camping resort.

In 1974 I met a nurse named Jean. As we became better acquainted, we began discussing the possibility of going into a business that would provide mammograms in the Canadian medical system. This was her expertise. I would provide the financial backing. Eventually, I learned that Canada would not allow me, a non-citizen, to be a part of their health care system.

Jean had been invited to visit some friends that summer in Jamaica and invited me to meet her there. Her friends had a son and daughter who were away for the summer. I was invited to stay in the son's room.

I flew to the Bahamas from Cleveland in my Boeing 707. There I connected with a commercial flight to Jamaica. According to my instructions from Jean, I was to drive from the airport in north Jamaica to a 1,000-acre ranch in southwest Jamaica. The drive was long and the sun was starting to set. I began to worry. I had heard that a lot of criminal acts were happening most evenings there, and this family had four Rhodesian Ridgeback dogs for protection. They were brown, big, and powerful.

Finally, there was the driveway as the sun was about to set. Two of their dogs met me, so I stayed in the car until the owner came out to escort me into the home. Once I was in the house, the dogs accepted me.

Whenever I arose in the morning, I was told to just go to the large porch facing the ranch and the maid would bring my breakfast and lunch. Dinner was served when everyone was together.

What a view from the porch: they had a thousand head of cattle, their own plane, a landing strip and a river that provided pure drinking water. The only negative was that the country had recently become socialist. All company boards of directors had to have a majority of government politicians on the board. The government controlled every business. This couple was regularly flying their valuables out of the country in their plane. The wife was an American citizen and the husband was an English citizen. During the day they would butcher their cattle. In the late evening the local butcher would pick up the meat that was butchered that day. I watched as thousands of American dollars were counted out each night on the living room coffee table. A few months later there were no more cattle.

Each afternoon, at four p.m., we had tea by the river. Again, I was spoiled thanks to another friendship. Jean and I were able to play some tennis and visit a major outdoor farmers' market about thirty minutes drive from the home. Eventually, the couple sold the ranch and left the country. The money from the sale was not allowed to leave the country. Years later, when Jamaica was no longer socialist, they were able to retrieve the money.

> **"Curiosity can lead to new experiences and learning."**
> **—Unknown**

CHAPTER 14

SHOPPING CENTER CONSTRUCTION

One of my law school classmates, Gene, invited me to join him and four others in building medium-sized shopping centers (also called "strip malls"). Two of the six were lawyers, one was an architect, one was experienced in leasing, and another in building management. I was to be the finance person. This occurred in the mid-1970s.

When I joined the group, the first center was underway in northern Ohio. The property was secured by a lease-purchase agreement. The zoning had been approved. The corporation also had secured the agreements to build seven more similar centers in Pennsylvania.

The six of us each received 15 percent of the stock for $15,000. The remaining 10 percent of the stock was held within the corporation for future purposes (attracting personnel, bonuses to people performing above and beyond expectations, etc.).

Soon the center was fully leased and a contractor was selected. His quote was $1,450,000. With this price and the leases in hand, I went shopping for a construction loan. My success came through the father of a high school buddy, Dale. His father lived in Florida and was on the board of a savings and loan company there. The loan was to be for $1,500,000, leaving us an additional $50,000 for working capital.

A few days before the contractor began framing and pouring cement, the Federal Reserve Bank—ignorantly, in my opinion—raised the prime rate as high as 12 percent in 1974 and 20 percent in 1980 and 1981. That increased commercial and home loans to the range of 17 percent to 25 percent. Their intent was to boost the economy. The result was the reverse. Many contractors across the country filed for bankruptcy. Our contractor said he needed another $200,000 before he could start because of the excess interest he would have to pay.

Upon presenting this to our lender in Florida, they were willing to increase the loan if the tenant leases would be increased accordingly. None of the tenants would agree to the increase. As a result we were stopped in our tracks. This also stopped many of the construction projects across the country—thanks again to the incompetence of big government and small-minded politicians.

Also lost to us were the next seven strip malls in Pennsylvania.

On Perseverance: "You may have to fight a battle more than once to win it."
—**Margaret Thatcher,** *British Prime Minister*

On Opportunity: "When one door closes, another door opens; but we so often look so long and so regretfully upon the closed door that we do not see the ones which open for us."
—**Alexander Graham Bell,** *Inventor*

"A vision without a task is but a dream; a task without a vision is drudgery. A vision and a task are the hope of the world."
—**Author unknown**

"You don't always have control over what happens, but you do have control over what you do with the experience."
—**Author unknown**

CHAPTER 15

PUNA PRINTERS

During the time I was involved in the businesses reviewed in chapters eleven and twelve, I received a phone call from my friend Carla. The month was January. She said to me, "I'm sick and tired of this fuckin' city [Cleveland], and I'm going to Honolulu." "What are you going to do there?" I asked her. "I don't know!" she said. My follow-up comment was that my friend John had just bought a franchise called Sir Speedy Instant Printing Center, and he was very happy with it. "Would you like to see it?" I asked. Carla was quite interested and I made an appointment to have John show us his shop. Actually Carla had been thinking of some kind of franchise. After the tour of John's shop, Carla was ready to get the same franchise in Honolulu.

Yes, Carla's comment to me represented a lot of anger. She was the top salesperson for a nationwide company. In fact, her sales were double that of the next salesperson consistently, year after year. When annual raise time came around, she would get $10. The reason was that she would not sleep with her boss. In fact, she took the card representing the $10 raise and threw it on her boss's desk while saying, "You can keep this raise; it isn't worth reprogramming your fuckin' machine."

Luck was with Carla, though: the Honolulu Sir Speedy franchise was available. The terms were $35,000 up front and $15,000 working capital. After selling her small home, she could only raise $25,000 for investment. Knowing that Carla was a record-setting salesperson, an ex-school teacher and financially responsible, I offered to put up the additional $25,000 for a one-half ownership of the new corporation. Also on my mind was a legal opportunity to visit Hawaii as a business expense in the future to "check on one of my investments."

As anticipated, Sir Speedy called us about four months later to say they were ready for our two weeks of schooling at their offices in Newport Beach, California.

The training was intense; it was every day for fourteen days along with ten evenings. During that time, the Sir Speedy representatives were in Honolulu to find the best location, receive the equipment package (press, cutter, folder, shelving, counter, etc.), and hire our first employee (a press operator).

After "graduation," we flew to Honolulu. Carla located an apartment and settled in. I stayed one week in a hotel (since I had no intention of living in Hawaii). My task was to locate an attorney to form the corporation and teach Carla the minimum bookkeeping necessary so that I could prepare financial statements each month in Cleveland. Also, during this week, I located a used Ford Escort station wagon with which the deliveries could be made.

After the first year of business we were not receiving the promised continuing support from Sir Speedy. I called a vice president at Sir Speedy, who I had befriended earlier, and registered my disappointment. Fortunately, he leveled with me. Sir Speedy was growing so fast that it needed $500,000 more in financing. Their business bank president didn't like the very aggressive Sir Speedy president and was holding back on the loan. And our distance from the mainland compounded our problem.

Appreciating our situation, the vice president made me a great offer. He encouraged me to write the vice president a strongly worded letter and request a complete disassociation with Sir Speedy.

He would then respond with negative firmness, according to company policy. Then, on his own, the vice president would write us off their records and we would never hear from them again. Also, we would no longer have to pay them 5 percent of our sales.

After that ordeal we, of course, had to drop the Sir Speedy name. We replaced it with our street name "Puna" and became Puna Printers.

From that point forward, the business was showing steady growth thanks to

Carla's management and sales savvy.

Fast-forward three years to 1977. My net worth dropped from being a millionaire to being more or less broke because of the way the businesses in chapters thirteen and fourteen ended.

So what now? My decision was to move to Hawaii and contribute to the growth of Puna Printers. With no income, I arrived in Honolulu in June carrying my sleeping bag and the minimum amount of clothing. I slept on the counter of the print shop for three months, using the shop toilet and sink room to "bathe." I was able to budget three meals a day on four dollars: a $1 breakfast, $1 lunch and $2 dinner. My salary was $200 per month. I had use of the shop delivery wagon for transportation. I wouldn't qualify for social security for at least fifteen more years.

Working daily with my partner Carla was much different emotionally than when we knew each other as friends in Ohio. Since I had a lot to learn about all aspects of the shop, I was treated as a lesser employee—less than the press operator and the counter person. According to Carla, "I moved too slow."

After about two and a half months of this, we decided to separate. Carla bought my half for about 20 percent more than my original investment. The payback included 10 percent down and approximately $500 monthly on the balance for five years. The negotiations to reach this settlement were not smooth. We had no buyback agreement, and each of us owned 50 percent, which was not a very workable situation. At the golf driving range, this had all been prearranged. It was certainly my bad for not planning as well as before, but I did enter this under different circumstances that clouded my mind. In the future, I either would want 51 percent or, if that was not possible, perhaps each party could get 49 percent with 2 percent in the hands of an agreed upon mediator.

I left to open my own shop in the other side of town.

"The greatest thing in this world is not so much where we are, but in what direction we are moving."
—**Oliver Wendell Holmes Jr.,** *U. S. Supreme Court Justice*

On Success: "Achievement is largely the product of steadily raising one's levels of aspiration . . . and expectation."
—**Jack Nicklaus,** *Golfer*

Chapter 16

Kapiolani Printers

P una Printers was on the west side of town (*ewa* in Hawaii) so I opened my shop on the east side of town, (Diamond Head) on Kapiolani Boulevard. I named it Kapiolani Printers. This allowed potential customers to recognize at a glance what we did (and where we were located). Other shops in town used names like "Kailua Imaging," "Newtech Graphics," and "Graphic Designs." They would not be my first choice if I were looking for a print shop.

With the down payment from the sale of Puna Printers, I was able to rent an on-street location and buy used equipment (press, folder, cutter, etc.). Kapiolani Printers was soon open for business. For living quarters, I was able to rent a small room for just $150 per month with a shared bathroom in a house shared by four parties. The monthly payments from Carla covered my rent, used company auto, and living expenses. I was able to eat for four dollars a day

Lunch and dinner usually included a lot of macaroni and rice.

I created a financial projection (budget) for the first year (see Figure 1). With all expenses listed I needed sales of $4,800 per month to break even. I budgeted $2,500 in sales for the first month, $3,500 for the second month, $4,500 for the third month, $5,200 for the fourth month and $6,000 for the fifth month.

Figure 1. Financial Budget Projection

SALES: MONTHLY 4000 2500 5000

COST OF SALES

PAPER	15%	800	550	1000
CAMERA + PRESS SUPPLIES	—	160	100	200
OUTSIDE SVCS	— 5	200	125	250
COPIER	1½	80	70	100
MAINT		300	300	300
TOTAL COSTS		1540	1145	1850
GROSS MARGIN		2460	1355	3150

EXPENSES:

2ND PRESSMAN

COUNTER	300	—	600
PRESS MGR	1000	1000	1000
FICA + WORK COMP	70	70	70
ADVTG - SALES PROMO	350	350	350
RENT	630	630	630
PHONE	80	80	80
OFFICE SUPPLIES - POSTAGE	40	25	50
INS + MMBA	40	40	50
INTEREST	—	—	—
PROFESSIONAL FEES			
MISC			
TOTAL EXPENSES	2460	2145	2800
P or (L)	-0-	(790)	+350

Actual Sales

a. Month 1—$3,000
b. Month 2—$4,000
c. Month 3—$5,200
d. Month 4—$6,000
e. Month 5—$7,000

As you can see, Kapioilani Printers was profitable by the end of the third month. During those first three months, I was outside the shop all day making sales calls. After that I came back into the shop to help with the expanding business. In addition, rather than hiring another employee, I made all the deliveries to customers during the day and worked in the evening until eleven p.m. doing tasks such as folding, collating, cutting, and binding.

When I started budgeting, I didn't stop with one budget. I would review it every week for the first couple of months. Every three to six months thereafter I would review the prior budget and make adjustments based on what changes seemed appropriate. These changes would include the possibility of needing another employee, adjusting for rising costs, or anticipating the addition of another piece of equipment.

Your major challenges in running a business are not limited to balancing income to expense for the purpose of gaining profitability. The employees can be just as challenging. The following are three examples.

[1] During my second year in business, I hired a local man to handle deliveries. And, at that time, I appointed my top pressman, Rog, to manager of the shop. His ability as a pressman was unsurpassed. In order to have him feel he had a home with Kapiolani Printers, I offered him 30 percent of the corporation stock. He would earn 6 percent of the stock at the end of each year for five years. If he left or was fired before the end of the entire five years, the option became totally invalid.

A couple months later, the deliveryman was very late in returning to the shop after his short delivery schedule. When questioned, he said he had been involved in an accident with another car.

Upon further inquiry I learned that he had periodic problems with blacking out. He seemed surprised when I said he could not drive the delivery vehicle anymore. Coincidently, earlier that day, one client paid his bill with four $100 bills. At the end of the day, when counting the proceeds, the $400 was missing.

The next morning I told Rog I thought the ex-deliveryman stole the money. The manager came up with every excuse to prove me wrong. I also did not appreciate Rog trying to cover for the deliveryman by saying somebody must have broken into the shop that night. There was no evidence to indicate a break-in.

I had a sheriff friend visit the ex-deliveryman's home. His older sister was home and said she would question her brother when he got home, and then call me in a day or two. She did that. Her brother admitted to stealing the money. He agreed to pay back the $400 at the rate of twenty dollars per week. After two weeks, there were no more payments. The cost to legally follow up was prohibitive... and the loss was charged off.

[2] A bindery man, while operating the folding machine, said the noise was bothering his ears. I then supplied him with protective ear covers. He continued to complain and said he wanted to go to the worker's compensation office. I learned he had been going to pistol and rifle ranges for years, which harmed his hearing. Therefore, I cautioned him not to file a claim. Upon his return, he said he did not file a claim. I called the worker's compensation office to learn what had taken place. In truth, he had filed a claim. I immediately had the claim quashed upon relating the firing range history.

A few months later, this bindery person managed to "sprain" his wrist while carrying a carton of ten reams of 20-pound 8 ½ x 11 paper. I was unaware of the incident. He filed a claim with the worker's compensation office. The outcome was that he was awarded $15,000 from my insurance company and a monthly compensation from my worker's compensation fund. All of this came to my attention when he quit his job. He flew to California, bought a cheap pickup, and got into the business of delivering drugs in southern California.

When I relayed this to the worker's compensation office and requested them to cease the monthly check, they said no. They would have to hear from the recipient.

[3] A male graphic artist in the shop named Joe had a runny nose almost every day. I said to him finally, "That is some cold you have." Joe indicated he believed there was a virus in the window air-conditioners.

So I hired, at substantial cost, a company to test and sanitize my air-conditioners. No virus was detected. Fortunately, with my agreed privacy, another employee said Joe's problem was the regular sniffing of cocaine. When I shared with Joe the information about his coke habit, he denied it—but did quit on his own soon thereafter.

One of my first customers was a new time-share sales company. Their first order was disappointingly small: 100 three-part forms and 100 one-sided forms. I drove a mile to their office.

But, within one year, their printing needs were in excess of $5,000 per month; they continued at that level for many years thereafter. After one and a half years, I had to hire a second pressman and another counter/bindery person. Near the end of the second year, I acquired another shop location, one more pressman, and one more counter/bindery person. This counter/bindery person, Terry—whom I have mentioned earlier—would soon become the shop manager. Terry would remain in that position for almost ten years.

When I acquired the second shop location, Rog was still my shop manager. I assigned him to manage the new shop and call on prospective customers in that area. For this shop I bought a large Xerox copy machine that would allow us to also compete for large copy jobs. Several times when I stopped by this new shop, Rog was not there. Eventually, I learned that he was working on opening his own shop… while on my payroll. I had to fire him. This also terminated his stock options.

About a week later, I received a call from his attorney. This attorney said in a menacing manner, "When are you going to pay Rog for the part of the stock option he had earned?" "Did you read the agreement thoroughly?" I asked the attorney. After he had admitted he had not, I said, "When you thoroughly read the agreement, please call me if you have any more questions." He did not know I had a law degree, had drawn up this agreement, and wouldn't be frightened by his tone of voice. I never heard from him again. If I didn't have a law degree, I would have had him call my lawyer.

The shop space I rented included an adjacent storefront next door that I could rent to another business. A known graphic artist came in the shop and said he would like to rent the space. Tom said that he could not pay rent for about six months, but could we work out a deal. I allowed him to use the space in return for some graphic work now and then. We signed a simple agreement to this effect. During his second month, a talented young female artist named Sue came by looking for Tom. She wanted to be his understudy for no pay. By Tom's fourth month, he had a major project under way. Sue had quickly improved her talent. Soon thereafter, her attorney boyfriend sued Tom for compensation for Sue (even though she had never expected any pay and was very happy with her free lessons). The lawsuit was filed and served against Tom; and I was listed as a party to the suit.

Be aware that anyone can sue anyone else just by filing papers in court. And never ignore a filing. If you don't hire an attorney to answer the suit, you can lose by default.

Sue's attorney was very competent. He sued for $1,100 in 'back' wages. I had to bring my attorney since I was included in the suit. The judge held for Sue. Tom had no money. In Hawaii the courts have a "deep pocket" rule: they go after anyone with money that has any association with the defendant. Since Tom was my "tenant" (even with free use of the space), I was forced to pay the $1,100 judgment. After one year, Tom moved to larger quarters.

The attorney representing me was my regular attorney's assistant. My regular attorney was in court in another lawsuit. When I received his bill of $1,200, I rebelled. We settled for $300. Even a good faith gesture can cost you in some jurisdictions.

A year later I rented the space to Glen, a dealer in gold and silver. Soon after, he said he wanted to sell his home and asked me to look at it. To humor him, I did (thinking there was no way I could buy a home at the time). The price was $140,000 for about 2,400 square feet on a hillside with great views of Diamond Head Mountain and Honolulu Airport (from the wraparound porch). Included were separate living quarters on a lower level (under the main house). Glen wanted 50 percent down (that is what he had invested). I fell in love with the house, but could only come up with $25,000 to $30,000. What to do? Coincidence? Maybe not!

I received a phone call from my Arthur Treacher's Fish & Chip partner. He decided to sell the East Coast stores since they were not growing, as did his Ohio stores. He also asked where he could mail my check for $45,000. Amazing! With that I could buy the house.

In chapter five I mentioned my first IRS audit. During the next three or four years in Honolulu I had two more audits. First an agent called me to come into his office in downtown Honolulu for "just a few simple questions." The questions eventually escalated to, "What do you do with the company car at night?" "This is beyond a simple question," I said. "You will have to deal with my CPA for anymore questions." I gave him my CPA's name and phone number and said good-bye. I was using the company car also as my personal car, which could be taxable to me and not fully deductible as a business expense.

Upon immediately calling my CPA, he said "Put your name and home phone number on the main door of the business under the words "In Case of Emergency Call." This, according to him, made it okay to take the company car home in the evening. The car is the only way I can return to the office in a hurry.

The next audit seemed more serious. Four quarters in a row I received a notice from the IRS saying I owed small amounts between thirty-five and seventy-nine dollars. I knew this was false since my CPA had set up my payment schedule and I was current on every payment. Then I received the fifth quarterly notice letter with two words in the upper left corner in red ink. Upon inquiring, I learned this meant the IRS was going to put a tax lien on everything I owned in about two or three weeks. I was under enough stress without this. In a temporary fit of rage, I wrote over this letter in red ink using every swear word I knew. I damned their machines, their letters, as well as the department itself, and returned the letter to the IRS in Fresno, California. Within ten days I had a phone call from a very pleasant IRS lady who said, "May I help you?" What a surprise.

"Yes, you may. I don't owe anything and am fed up with all these notices."

She was very understanding and told me of a new service just set up in downtown Honolulu. It is like a concierge in a hotel. If I go there, they have all my records and will help solve any problems. I could hardly believe my ears. I went there and they were expecting me. They told me that they would get back to me within ten days. They did exactly that. And I learned that they owed *me* money for each quarter. I don't recommend you do what I did, but a couple times I've erupted and gained the results I wanted (when I knew I was right).

When you have a small business with two or three employees, you may be less diligent with government posters. But, for my shop, I had to post state and federal posters regarding workers' compensation and unemployment insurance. Also, it became appropriate to create an employee work rules manual. With Terry as manager, we spent a couple days outside the shop and created and eighteen-page employee manual. Each employee was given a copy, and each employee had to sign the "original" copy acknowledging that they had received and had read their copy.

Also, by this time, I could afford and did take all my employees to dinner once a month. Everyone appreciated meeting in a relaxed environment like that.

A few paragraphs back I briefly mentioned using a sheriff. I met him one day when I had to pick up something in the sheriff's office in Honolulu. He was mostly Chinese with some Filipino mixture. With his beard, he looked like the old detective Charlie Chan, but with a stare that would stop you in your tracks. He overheard that I was from a print shop, started a conversation and said he was available to assist in collections if I had some "deadbeats." He liked to be called Pete. His capability was exceptional. One time a client owed me $700, but was elusive. Each time I thought I found his whereabouts, he was gone. I called Pete. About three days later I get a call from Pete in Waikiki saying, "Your client wants to talk to you." When the client got on the line, I could tell he was frightened. He said, "I'll pay. I'll pay right now. Please tell this collector to go away and leave me alone!" I had to chuckle. Pete affected people that way.

By 1981 I purchased my first computer: a TRS80 model 3, with forty-eight kilobytes of memory. It cost me $2,400. The software for a print shop was $5,000. It would print quotes for customers for different quantities (e.g., 100, 500, 1,000, etc.). It also did some bookkeeping. In addition, the software was to carry forward each month's bookkeeping, combining them for quarterly and annual reports. That wasn't happening. The software developer (from Washington State) didn't believe me that the accumulation was not working. He returned to Honolulu to show me how it worked. He couldn't get it to work either. Terribly frustrated (and I guess despondent), he returned home and committed suicide. I was his sales representative in Hawaii and did not have to come up with the $5,000 for the software. At least I could print out quotations for customers.

The next year I bought the best fax machine on the market at that time. The cost: $6,800. Really!! I was only the third person in Honolulu who offered fax service at that time. But, a fax cost $10 plus long distance charges. One day an attorney came in needing fifty pages of a signed contract faxed to the mainland. His bill was approximately $590.

By now the shop was averaging over $30,000 each month in sales with a staff of twelve. Then there was a bump in the road of progress. I received an eviction notice; the property was sold and a high-rise condo was to be built. My move is covered in chapter seventeen.

It was 1983, and I had not had a vacation since I arrived in Hawaii in 1977. A lady named Tiff tempted me with a special advertisement: fly to Tahiti for two weeks for $450, lodging included. Not only did that get my attention, but my employees also thought that was a good idea. Soon there were stick-um notes on the wall in front of my desk: "Away is Good." They all were right; it was time for me to get away and relax.

Soon I was landing at Faa airport in Papeete, Tahiti. It was July and the lodging was in a high school dormitory with double-deck beds set up in a gym-sized room with about twenty showers at one end of the area. The students were away for summer vacation. I spent most of the first week exploring the city of Papeete and the island of Tahiti. But then the outer islands beckoned. We flew to some islands and took a ferryboat to other islands. Altogether I visited Moorea, Raiatea, Tahaa, Bora Bora, and Huahine. In Papeete I met and became good friends with one of the best-known men in town, a man named Teva Sylvain. He was *the* photographer. He also printed (using his photos) most all of the postcards and calendars that were on sale for tourists in Tahiti and all over France. Tahiti is under French control—that is why it is also referred to as French Polynesia.

When Teva came to Honolulu for business, I was able to produce a few favors for him. On my seven return visits to Tahiti, I got to stay sometimes at his lovely home on the ocean and use his jet ski right from his dock.

When I returned to Honolulu after this vacation, I was more tanned and rested than ever before or since. My employees continued to remind me, "Away is Good."

At this point I did some TV advertising and would still make personal calls when requested. There were many print shops in the Honolulu area, ranging from quick print shops to large commercial print companies. However, I managed to attract some special jobs that could easily have gone to a large commercial printer. The reason was our service and ingenuity.

One day I received—as did perhaps every other printer in Honolulu—a request in the mail for a bid on an eight-page newspaper in five languages for five days for the National Cash Register Company (NCR). The newspaper would include many photos and be delivered to three Waikiki hotels by seven a.m. each day. NCR had planned to come to Hawaii to celebrate their 100th worldwide anniversary convention. I envisioned how we could do it for a good price to NCR and a very good profit for Kapiolani Printers. But, of course, I couldn't perform the work on our small presses, which printed 8 ½ x 11, 8 ½ x 14, and 11 x 17 precut sheets.

I obtained a bid and commitment from a friend with a large printing press.

Then I got a commitment from each language department at the University of Hawaii to translate the articles into French, German, and Spanish starting at one p.m. each day for five days. I would deliver the copy and pick it up after the translation, two hours later. My staff did the typesetting in-house. The Japanese was translated by a Japanese specialty shop and returned to us all typeset in Japanese characters by six p.m.

Now, with a staff of sixteen, hours were split with six working from five p.m. to midnight. Terry worked the late shift and delivered the final paste-up pages each night to the printer. The large press printer completed the printing, folding, and seven a.m. delivery.

The coordination was exceptional. NCR was so pleased they even suggested that I add a substantial bonus to our bill. They were well aware what the cost would have been with a commercial printer (at least double our final billing).

Another exceptional printing experience occurred in 1987. There is a Variety Club in Hawaii, founded in 1966 in Honolulu. Entertainers in Pittsburgh formed the first Variety Club in 1927. As the Club expanded, their fundraising events assisted thousands of children's institutions all over the world.

When Dolly Parton decided to build a restaurant in Hawaii Kai, Oahu, Hawaii, the Variety Club promoted a fundraiser recognizing Dolly. Many companies in Honolulu contributed their time, talents, and products to support the fundraiser. My company offered to contribute the printing of the tickets for a Celebrity Masquerade Ball fundraiser to be held October 31, 1987, at Dolly's new restaurant in Hawaii Kai. It was called Dockside Plantation. I also printed the program for a luncheon fundraiser held October 4 at the Hilton Hawaiian Village Hotel.

The grand opening party at Dolly's Dockside Plantation restaurant was electrifying and memorable. There were so many great costumes. I had a full beard at the time; I put a bandana around my head and appeared as Willie Nelson. When I arrived and stepped out of a limousine, Dolly greeted me with a big hug while exclaiming, "Willie!" Life doesn't get much better than that. I had a professional photographer in the crowd to take pictures. Dolly and I hugging was one of my favorites.

Two years later Honolulu's prestigious weekly, the *Pacific Business News,* profiled me. The half-page review was titled: "Terry Tries Not to Copy the Competition." This was a pleasant surprise since I was not one to seek notability.

My business expanded each year. When I sold it in 1994, it was grossing over $60,000 per month in three locations with twenty-two employees. The sales price was $400,000, payable at the rate of $5,000 per month with no interest.

Critique

The sale of Kapiolani Printers was not a wise sale. It was a sale made when I was under a high level of stress and I wanted out. Around this time, my bed and breakfast was unraveling (see chapter twenty), as well as the business building in chapter seventeen. This was due to the extreme drop in real estate values in Hawaii; both properties were lost to foreclosure. This was a poor time to handle a major decision. I didn't think of consulting another sizeable business owner for suggestions.

I sold Kapiolani Printers to a sister and brother, Bea and Ned. Bea had been operating a very successful print shop in downtown Honolulu for years, and I was confident in her ability. Her brother was the unknown, and I should have had a clause limiting wages for a couple years, or until I received a substantial pay down (50 percent) on the selling price. I assumed—yes, a bad thing to do—that Bea would have some common sense control over her brother. That didn't happen. Ned took control, set Bea's salary at $5,000 per month and his at $9,000 per month. Then Ned hired a so-called marketing expert (his friend) at $7,500 per month. I never paid myself more than $4,000 per month in order to build reserves.

About six months after the sale, I heard that Ned was going to file bankruptcy for the print shops. I forcefully took back my shops and resold what remained for about $70,000, payable over ten years. What I didn't receive was not a total loss. The approximate $300,000, under the tax code, was considered an operating loss (which can be offset against any future earned income), as opposed to a capital loss (which can only be offset against capital gains). And it did happen that way in chapter twenty-one.

On Persistence: "I do not think that there is any other quality so essential to success of any kind as the quality of perseverance. It overcomes almost everything, even nature."
—**John D. Rockefeller,** *Oil Executive*

On Integrity: "Live so that you wouldn't be ashamed to sell the family parrot to the town gossip."
—**Will Rogers,** *Humorist*

CHAPTER 17

THE WARD AVENUE BUSINESS BUILDING

The storefront location where I started Kapiolani Printers was part of an old warehouse. The entire corner property was purchased by a developer who planned and built a twenty-five–story condominium complex. This forced me to relocate after about four years in that location.

Just two blocks away was a corner building to which I could relocate. It also was on a busy street and had double my present floor space. At $4,000 a month, rent was much higher. This additional space allowed me to purchase a large dark-room camera from another printer going out of business. That enabled us to reduce costs by producing our own stats and veloxes.

Finally, Kapiolani Printers was a full-service print shop under one roof: printing, faxing, copying, typesetting, graphic art, and a dark room with the eight-foot–long camera.

My landlord was a man in his eighties and in very poor health. After one year as a tenant, the landlord asked me if I would be interested in buying the building. My answer was a quick "Yes," and we tentatively agreed on $500,000 for this fee simple building. Fee simple (owning the land as well as the building) was rare in Honolulu. Most land was leased from large estates, including land under homes. You might "own" your home, but you paid lease rent on the land every month to an estate. The largest estate at the time was the Bishop Trust.

Before my landlord and I completed the sale/purchase transaction, he heard that someone else was willing to pay $575,000 for the property. Because I had first right of refusal in the rental agreement, he sued me to get out of the obligation so he could sell at the higher price. In court, before the trial, we agreed to settle on $535,000.

In addition, he wanted the closing on a specified date. This puzzled me at first. Then it became clear: it was a tax savings. If he died after closing, he and his wife would have a large capital gain tax. If he died before closing, she would inherit the property with a "cost to her" equal to the current value—the sale price. Therefore, the proceeds from the sale would equal her cost of acquiring the property and, voila, no capital gains tax.

That is what occurred. He disconnected his own life support system and died. In effect, I was buying the property from his wife. Yes, he hated the IRS that much.

When I sold the print shop, I did not include the building (which was in my name and separate from the business). My mortgage payment was $5,000 per month. I rented the building to two chiropractors for $10,000 per month.

About six months after the chiropractors moved in, they indicated an interest in buying the building. We agreed upon a price of $1,000,000 and a down payment of $400,000. These potential purchasers were active in buying and selling real estate in Hawaii (what we would now call "flipping" properties), and making good profits. They liquidated a couple of properties, and one of my tenants accumulated $400,000 in his checking account to cover the down payment.

The sale did not happen! As soon as the money was in his account, his wife sued for divorce and emptied the account. The chiropractors continued to rent the building until their lease expired. I lost out on a very timely sale.

"You don't understand anything until you learn it more than one way."
—Marvin Minsky, *Mathematician*

Chapter 18

Letterpress Print Shop

According to Webster's Dictionary, "letterpress" is the process of printing directly from an inked, raised surface upon which the paper is impressed; this is also called relief printing.

The oldest machine in the shop I bought was over 100 years old and still in use. It was called Linotype. It formed one line of type by setting one letter at a time in a trough. These single letters were made of a hard metal (like brass) in relief so they could withstand the molten lead poured over them. When cooled, this lead line of type could be set in a press frame with other lines of type. Once the frame was complete, it could be attached to a special press like the Heidelberg presses in my shop. Because of the softness of the lead, the print jobs were "short run"—usually five to five hundred copies.

These presses are also used to die cut, foil stamp, and emboss work done by regular printing companies. It would not be cost effective for regular print shops to do their own letterpress work since only a small percentage of regular printing requires what a letterpress shop can do.

The letterpress shop I bought had been in business for many years and was named American Press. It had been in bankruptcy for about eighteen months. The owner was a good friend and I asked if I could buy the shop. He said he could arrange for me to buy the business if he could still have a job with the company. I agreed.

The company debt was about $150,000. After reviewing the accounting records, I could not see any reason for this company to be in bankruptcy. My offer had to be accepted by the bankruptcy court. I offered and they accepted $50,000 cash. For this price I acquired an established business, four small Heidelberg presses, one very large Heidelberg press, the Linotype, the offices, the employees, and the lease for the location.

I brought the owner of another letterpress shop in as a partner. He accepted 49 percent of the company for 49 percent of the $50,000. His was looking at an eviction from his location since a developer purchased an entire block just one block from Ala Moana Center. Not only was this perfect for him, but it provided me with an ideal buyer for my 51 percent if I wanted to sell some time in the future. Also, this partner had been in this business for over thirty years. I could learn a lot from him. He was the ideal partner, being an easy person to be around and work with. That was more good luck.

Our takeover was planned for January 1 of the following year. I purposely made no changes to the shop or the operation since the accounting didn't indicate any reason for being bankrupt. American Press was doing about $25,000 in business each month. At the end of the first month, there was a net profit of $5,000 (20 percent of sales), just as I had anticipated. Upon more research, I learned that the prior owner was heavily skimming from his own company. During his bankruptcy, he bought his new wife a new Cadillac and paid cash. This gave me cause to keep a close eye on his actions.

This was a non-union shop (as were all my other businesses). After about four months, one of the longtime employees talked the other employees into voting in a union. And so they did. My response was to immediately pay them union wages. The employees soon realized that not only were union wages less than what I had been paying them, but they also had to pay union dues. After about three more months, the union was voted out.

The shop was not in perfect repair when I took over. Even one electrical wire was not properly protected. Immediately I brought in an electrical company to go over the entire shop and also do some rewiring so as to reduce our electrical bill. At about the same time I got a visit from a female federal government employee. She said that she would have the entire shop checked for safety. By the time she was done I would be charged some very heavy fines. How could she say that without the results of her inspection? She was scheduled to start her safety check the next day. When I told her I had electricians presently working in the building, she almost exploded with disappointment. "Well, let me know when they are done. I can't do anything as long as they are here." Without realizing at the time, I had a trump card. Hooray!

When the electricians were finished, I notified the Fed lady. After spending several days in the shop, she couldn't come up with anything for which to fine me. She appeared quite angry as she departed. I sensed that one of my employees must have tipped off the government.

Even though I was the controlling owner, as I learned to do from the venture in chapter fifteen, I treated my partner as I would have wanted to be treated. I did nothing regarding the company without notifying him first. I provided complete transparency. That way our trust of each other would continue to grow.

Eventually, I did sell him my 51 percent for a gain of 100 percent (a total of $51,000).

"One man practicing sportsmanship is far better than fifty preaching it."
—**Knute Rockne,** *Football Coach*

"Even if you're on the right track, you'll get run over if you just sit there."
—**Will Rogers,** *Humorist*

CHAPTER 19

PERSONALIZED GIFTS

Prior to selling my print shops, I met a man named Jerry. He was about thirty, aggressive, and owned a small personalized gift showroom with samples of hundreds of gift items. A gift item included almost anything you could print or etch, or upon which you could place a name or logo (cups, pens, towels, hats, glasses, folders, etc.). I purchased letter openers and magnetic calendars from him to advertise my print shop.

He contacted me after I sold my shops since I had already expressed an interest in that business. His workforce included his wife and one employee. A friend of mine, Cori, also wanted to be involved. The corporation stock was therefore divided as follows: 40 percent to Jerry and his wife; 20 percent each to Cori, Soto, the existing employee, and me.

In order to more quickly grow the business, we decided to purchase another business like Jerry's that was larger and for sale. The price was $125,000. The sellers wanted cash. My bank was willing to loan the money. The volume of sales in the purchased business was five times the sales in Jerry's shop.

I had the banker go over the records of this larger gift company. I had my attorney prepare the buy/sell agreements. All appeared to be in order... until we took over. We then learned that many of the seller's clients had recently switched to another company. This was not evident during our due diligence, and was hidden by the seller.

We instituted a lawsuit against the sellers (a man and his wife). My attorney attempted to separate the lawsuit into two actions: a civil suit (which would be in arbitration) and a criminal suit. Unfortunately, a Hawaii law disallowed the separation since the civil suit was in arbitration instead of a civil court.

The arbitrator (judge) was the recognized expert in Hawaii (he had written *the* book on arbitration). The case was in arbitration daily (testimony in front of the judge for several hours each day) for about four weeks.

On Friday of the fourth week, there was a maximum of one day of testimony left. The arbitrator announced that he was going on vacation for two weeks. This was a total surprise. I knew that the seller still had $200,000 to $300,000 on deposit in this state and we wanted to attach the funds so as to satisfy our anticipated judgment. But the cash bond required was more than we could raise on short notice.

Two weeks later the arbitration was about the continue. The seller communicated to the arbitrator that his (the seller's) wife was very ill and he had to be with her. The arbitrator allowed another two-week delay. Two weeks later, there was another delay. The wife was close to death, we are told. By this time, the seller has transferred their bank deposits to another state.

Finally the arbitrator found in our favor. But the judgment was never satisfied since we couldn't locate the funds. And we were not allowed to bring a criminal action. The wife did die and the husband moved to another state. Jerry's business did continue (on a smaller scale) but was stressed financially while paying off the bank loan. Later Jerry and his wife separated. Cori moved to the mainland, and I bought a bed and breakfast on the Big Island. Eventually, Soto was left with the business.

CRITIQUE

I should have brought in a certified public accountant (CPA) to review the company I planned to purchase (instead of just a bank vice president). I *assumed* the bank VP had sufficient concern to look deeply into the records. My bad again. When a bank makes a loan to a successful past client, they are quite sure they will be repaid. A hired CPA has a greater responsibility. This was penny wise and pound foolish.

"Life is a school and you are here to learn. Problems are life's lessons from which you learn."
—**Unknown**

"Don't worry about it. Babe Ruth struck out on occasion, too."
—**Walter Annenberg,** *Publisher*

CHAPTER 20

BED AND BREAKFAST

The largest island in Hawaii goes by the same name but is also called the Big Island. On the southwest side of the island is the city of Kailua-Kona. It is where the main airport of the entire island is located. Hilo is the city on the southeast side. To the north is Waimea (Kamuela). On the coast east of Waimea is the town of Honokaa. My bed and breakfast was at the 2,000 feet level above Honokaa. It had commanding views of the ocean from the front of the property and of the mostly snow-covered mountain of Mauna Kea from the rear.

Friends of mine, Bill and Sue, wanted to move from the island of Oahu (where the city of Honolulu is located) to the Big Island. They hoped to locate a B & B and manage it if I would buy it. Bill and Sue spent many months exploring potential sites. Finally, they showed me one to which I was very attracted. It consisted of seven acres. On the property was a five-bedroom, three-bath home that was three years old, and a two-bedroom, one-bath cottage that was about one year old. If I purchased it, the mortgage and taxes would be $2,300 per month. The purchase price was $500,000 with a down payment of 20 percent.

Bill and Sue had four friends who also wanted to move with them to the Big Island, and would each pay $500 per month for their room. Bill and Sue made up the difference and signed an agreement to manage the property.

My friends had been active in the hospitality business for many years, and Sue was an experienced cook. The cottage would rent for $199 per night for the first night, including breakfast prepared by Sue. A week's rental would be $149 per night. Sue would also prepare other meals at up to $200 for two people. Also, upon request, Bill would drive our guests to and from the airport for an additional fee.

Any profits, over and above all expenses, would be split equally.

The driveways were not completed. Inquiring around the area, we located one of the most highly awarded rock and cement craftsmen in the world just two miles away. At first I just knew him as a "cement man." After finishing the driveway, Abe had several suggestions to upgrade the entrance of the property. Soon, we had a grand entrance framed with two seven-foot pillars made by wiring together six keawe logs, mounds of soil planted with a variety of local flowers, plants, and a log embankment on the left side as you enter the property. All of this cost just $1,600 because I listened to and respected his suggestions. Soon we were close friends.

Now I knew who he was. When the Hyatt Regency Waikoloa was built by 1988, he was awarded the bid to do all the rocks, waterfalls, and rivers on this enormous three-hotel property for $12 million. His bid was the highest, but he was the only one who could explain how he could keep the water clear, clean, and healthy. That job allowed him to retire.

Then Abe suggested a lava tube grotto and pool with a hot tub, with water jets inside the grotto and a waterfall over the entrance. For this he usually charged $40,000. My bill was only $12,500. I credited him for this grotto in my brochure. What I didn't know is that he entered my "grotto complex" in the annual worldwide competition for rock, river, and waterfall creations. Ours was awarded second place.

By late 1990, the B & B was in business as "Hawaii's Garden of Eden." We even had guests from Europe sign our guestbook, as well as many newlyweds. The cottage was totally secluded, and Bill and Sue were available to provide for their food and transportation needs. The newlyweds could totally relax and enjoy each moment together.

Until the Gulf War, the business was steadily expanding. With the advent of the war, tourism came to a crawl.

Then a major hurricane hit Hawaii. The damage was so great, most of the insurance companies left the state. This forced the State of Hawaii to create a Hurricane Fund to replace and act as an insurer for any further hurricanes. All property owners were assessed. I was billed approximately $750 per month. This raised my monthly overhead to over $3,000 per month.

About this time, Bank of America decided to enter the Hawaiian market. Among other disruptions, they bought up many savings and loan companies, including the one from which I borrowed money to do all the upgrades. At that time I was paying mostly interest and minimal principal. Bank of America immediately decided these loans should be paid off in three years—adding $2,000 to my monthly mortgage payment. Now my overhead is $5,000 per month.

There was more bad news. The banks in Japan started calling in all of their outstanding 0 percent to 1 percent mortgage loans. These loans allowed the Japanese to buy cheap property in Hawaii starting in the mid-1980s. Condos rose from $150,000 to $400,000 during a six- to seven-year period. The Japanese would fly to Honolulu, meet with a realtor, pick out ten or twelve homes/condos, write a check, and fly back to Japan. The recall on these loans forced a grand sale of the tens of thousands of properties purchased earlier. Real estate values plummeted, including my B & B and my million-dollar commercial site on Ward Avenue. My Ward Avenue renters lease ended, and they moved out. Because of the dismal business climate, I could not find another renter.

My B & B managers were having personal financial problems and their subrenters moved on. This meant they could not continue to manage the property and pay their agreed upon rental. With no one to replace them, I accepted a renter who could just pay $1,000 per month while looking after the property. But I still had mortgage payments of $10,000 per month for both properties.

In an attempt to recover, I condominiumized the seven acres. This resulted in a 2.5-acre lot with the cottage and a 4.5-acre lot with the five-bedroom house. I obtained a buyer for the smaller parcel for $139,000. Before I could close the sale, Bank of America foreclosed on the entire property.

A few years later, Bank of America completely vacated Hawaii (closing all branches), leaving behind many angry customers—including me. Just like today, the big banks have not done right by homeowners, most especially Bank of America. With the loss of the two properties due to foreclosure, I filed bankruptcy. My recovery is covered in chapter twenty-one.

Some of the losses due to the "grand sale" of properties by the Japanese and the subsequent plunge of the real estate market, were enormous. I recall the Hyatt Regency Waikoloa as the greatest loss. This HRW took eight years of planning and construction. It opened in 1988 at a cost of $288 million. HRW consisted of three hotel towers connected by a quarter-mile covered walkway, a Disney-style train next to the walkway, and a Disney-style boat next to that. Nearby was a large pond where you could swim with the dolphins. The quarter-mile walkway was lined with artifacts collected over four to five years throughout Asia. Its opening was so successful that it encouraged nineteen more investors to build nineteen more resort hotels in the islands. During 1991 and 1992, all nineteen opened and flooded the market. Subsequently they also were on the auction block. Ninety-five percent of the Hyatt Regency Waikoloa owners were Japanese. About 1995 they sold the HRW to Hilton Hotels for $55 million, a loss of $233 million.

On Risk: "Either you decide to stay in the shallow end of the pool or you go out in the ocean."
—Christopher Reeve, *Actor*

"Whenever the fear of losing wealth invaded my consciousness, I was able to remind myself of how little I really needed to be happy…. You can't control the economy. You can't control the forces that affect your business. But you can control your emotions."
—Mark Ford, *Investor*

CHAPTER 21

TIMESHARE SALES

In 1997 my friend Eileen invited me to Maui, Hawaii. She felt I would be successful in selling timeshares, and offered to train me. Actually, this had been on my mind for about eighteen years. At that earlier time I was doing the printing for one of the new timeshare companies in Hawaii and saw how much money some salespeople were making. Eileen had been selling timeshares for over twenty years, and was referred to as the "Queen of Timeshares."

By May 1997 I started selling for Consolidated Resorts, one of the oldest companies in the business in Hawaii. There was a lot of resistance to my being hired because of my age, which was sixty-seven at the time. Most of the sales people were in their twenties and thirties. By October I was awarded a plaque as salesman of the month. I was making more money than I ever paid myself in my businesses ($5,000 per month with no overhead). Our workday (five days each week) was from eight a.m. for a sales meeting; eight-thirty to nine a.m. to take our first "tour" (meet and make a presentation to prospects); by ten-thirty a.m. you had either made a sale or were ready for a second tour. Our workday was generally over by one p.m. By 1999 I was financially comfortable again. It was time for a vacation.

I enjoyed vacationing on cruise ships. When I learned I could have my own cabin and cruise almost for free, with the responsibility of dancing with the single women over fifty traveling alone, I applied. Fortunately for me, my sales manager encouraged me to take time off. My first such cruise was for forty-two days. I had to dance forty-five minutes before dinner, thirty minutes after dinner and thirty minutes after the evening show.

This first "Gentleman Host" trip embarked from Fort Lauderdale, Florida, and ended in Athens, Greece. Stops included several American coastal cities, Bermuda, and then across the Atlantic to Madeira, Morocco, Spain, Malta, Israel, Egypt, Santorini (Greece), Mykonos (Greece), Turkey, and arriving in Athens. What a way to see the world. This cruise was in January and February.

I repeated the "Gentleman Host" tour again in 2000 for forty-two days. This cruise began in Istanbul and ended in Copenhagen. We visited several resort cities bordering the Black Sea (Odessa, Sevastopol, and Yalta). Then it was off to Bulgaria, Malta, Sicily, Italy (Sorrento, Rome, Civitavecchia, and Genoa), Spain (Barcelona, Malaga, Cadiz, and Vigo), Portugal, Germany, France, England, Netherlands, Germany again, Sweden, Finland, and Russia on the way to Copenhagen. This cruise was in May and June.

In 2001 I took a fifty-two–day cruise from Singapore to Fort Lauderdale. In 2002 I took another fifty-two–day cruise from San Francisco to Singapore.

My fifth (and last) such cruise was for thirty-two days on a Silver Seas ship (290 passengers with 210 crewmembers). The cruise started in Manaus, Brazil, in November 2002 at the top of the Amazon River. After sailing down the Amazon River and stopping in each of the northern coast countries of South America, we visited Mexico and New Orleans. Then we sailed the Panama Canal to Puntarenas, Costa Rica. From there I flew home. One of the most amazing facts for me is that during the rainy season in Brazil, the Amazon River rises ninety feet (similar to a ten-story building).

By this time, Eileen changed companies and joined the Starwood Hotels and Resorts timeshare sales team. She became so impressed with the benefits and professionalism of Starwood that she encouraged me to apply. Again, because of my age, I went through the equivalent of ten interviews. Finally, by June 2003, I was hired to begin Starwood's sales training program in early July. The training encompassed four full weeks of memorizing a scripted presentation. The Starwood management adopted Dr. Moine's sales manual (*Unlimited Selling Power: How to Master Hypnotic Selling Skills*) as its "sales Bible."

As of the first of August, I was given my first tour. We would be selling a brand new timeshare resort that also opened August 1. Our presentations were not to exceed one hour and fifteen minutes. I was a little nervous—no, a lot nervous. My first two weeks I had no sales. The sales director told me later that he wondered if

I would succeed. In the next two weeks, I was closing sales on a par with the sales leaders of the newly trained sales team.

We were expected to sell about $200,000 in volume each month. If you did over $500,000 in sales in one month, the sales director took you to dinner the next month. I benefitted from that five or six times over the next two years.

With Consolidated Resorts, all salespeople were independent contractors (not an employee and no company benefits). With Starwood, we were not only employees, we had bonuses over and above commissions; stock options earned based upon sales volume; contributions to 401k; health insurance; and hotel points (based on sales volume), which could be used when staying at Starwood properties or exchanged for airline miles. Because of the stock options, I acquired several hundred shares of Starwood Hotels stock at a very reduced price.

During November 2004, I attended a two-day sales seminar given by Dr. Moine and Eric Lofholm in Los Angeles. That was very stimulating, and I returned to Maui supercharged. Three months later I set an office sales record: $751,350 of timeshare sales in one month. During my two years and four months with Starwood, I averaged an income of $20,000 per month. My total sales volume approximated $8 million.

Because of the "operating loss carry forward" as a result of the venture listed in chapter sixteen, I had no income tax liability on my first $300,000 of income.

What a great company! Thank you, Starwood Hotels.

In December 2005, I retired to Scottsdale, Arizona, bought a three-bedroom condo, and a red Mercedes.

On Individuality: "Differences can be a strength:"
—Condoleezza Rice, *Former U. S. Secretary of State*

On Opportunity: "When opportunity is close by, you have to drop everything and pursue it. The more you make those sacrifices, the better your chances of finding financial success."
—Dr. Steve Sjuggerud, *Investment Advisor*

Reward 8

After involvement with the venture in chapter twenty-one, and after retiring to Scottsdale in January 2006, I decided to take another cruise. The flight from Phoenix arrived in Buenos Aires, Argentina. I stayed a few days at one of Starwood Hotel's top fifty hotels, Park Tower, and toured the city. One evening I was thrilled by an Argentine steak dinner and a spirited flamenco dance show.

Later I boarded the Crystal Symphony for a sixteen-day cruise to Fort Lauderdale. The next stop was in Montevideo, Uruguay. I bought a couple bottles of Uruguayan wine and an artificial flower bouquet. Why the bouquet? The colors perfectly matched the sofa in my living room.

Next we docked in Rio de Janeiro. What a disappointing day; the rain flooded the entire city. I was told this was the first time in fifty years that the city had experienced such rain. That meant there would be no gawking at beautiful, bikini-clad women on their renowned Copacabana Beach. Even Sugarloaf Mountain was shrouded in fog.

Continuing on our northern route, there were one or two more stops in Brazil and many stops in the Caribbean, including Saint Lucia, Barbados, Guadeloupe, Saint Maarten, Saint Thomas and Puerto Rico. Too soon for my tastes, we were in Fort Lauderdale and departing the ship.

Reward 9

Sallie, the lady who was my dance/teaching partner in Honolulu for seventeen years, had always wanted to visit Japan during the annual Cherry Blossom Festival. On prior visits to Japan, she missed the special ten-day period during which the trees blossom.

Of interest to me at that time was to visit the Great Wall in China. I decided to combine both in a flight first to Beijing, China, from Honolulu, then return to Tokyo. In order to time the Cherry Blossom Festival, I researched with travel agents, the Internet, and the Japanese embassy.

This trip was approximately one and a half years prior to the Chinese Olympics. The air in Beijing was so polluted that during one day I could not see what was beyond two city blocks. My eyes watered and my nose was dripping when outside for just a few minutes. I thought to myself, *How can an Olympics be held in these conditions?*

While staying at a Sheraton Hotel in Beijing, I hired a car, driver, and guide for one day to take us to the Great Wall. The total cost was only about $110. The drive to the Great Wall from Beijing was more than one hour. At the Great Wall base, the guide had us board a ski lift to get to the top of the Wall. It is hard to comprehend that the Great Wall is over 2,000 miles long.

On the return flight to Tokyo, Mother Nature accommodated my schedule; we arrived just as the Cherry Blossoms had opened. Parks were filled with Japanese visitors enjoying the blossoms. Groups were partying on their eight-foot-by-twelve-foot square of blue plastic. A few blossoms were continually dropping like a mild snowfall. The days were sunny and warm. Japanese men's faces blushed profoundly after drinking almost any amount of alcohol.

Everything runs on time in Japan: trains, busses, and events. They have great organization. On this visit we stayed at the Sheraton next to Disneyland in Tokyo.

Glossary

ADMINISTRATIVE COURT——A body in the government to which the administration of justice is delegated. A body organized to administer justice, and including both judge and jury.

ARBITRATION ——The submission for determination of disputed matter to private unofficial persons selected in manner provided by law or agreement.

CIVIL LAW SUIT——The rule of action which every particular nation, commonwealth or city has established for itself; more properly called "municipal" law, to distinguish it from the "law of nature," and from international law.

COMMON STOCK——See PREFERRED STOCK.

CONDOMINIUM——Common ownership by two or more persons holding undivided fractional shares in the same property and having the right to alienate their shares resembling tenancy in common in Anglo-American law rather than joint tenancy with its rights of survivorship.

CONTRACT——Consensual: Founded on and completed by the mere agreement of the contracting, without any external formality or symbolic act to fix the obligation.

> **Real: It is necessary that there should be something more than mere consent, such as a loan of money, deposit, or pledge, which, from their nature, require a delivery of the thing.**

COMMODITY——In the commercial sense, any movable or tangible thing that is produced or used as the subject of barter or sale.

COOPERATIVE——Union of individuals to a common end (e.g., owning individual apartments in one building).

CORPORATION——An artificial person or legal entity created by or under the authority of the laws of a state or nation, ordinarily consisting of an association of numerous individuals who subsist as a body politic under a special denomination, which is regarded in law as having a personality and existence distinct from that of its several members, and which is, by the same authority, vested with the capacity of continuous succession, irrespective of changes in its membership.

CORPORATION BOND——A written promise by a corporation under seal to pay a fixed sum of money at some future time named, with stated interest payable at some fixed time or intervals, given in return for money or its equivalent received by the corporation, sometimes secured and sometimes not.

CRIMINAL LAW SUIT——An action or cause instituted to punish an infraction of the criminal laws. The proceeding by which a party charged with a public offense is accused and brought to trial and punishment.

DARK ROOM——A room freed from light or lighted by a safelight for handling or processing light-sensitive materials (as plates, films and paper).

DIE CUT——Use of cutting or shaping tools to create forms or outlines on paper or card stock in a letterpress shop.

DIRECTORS' MEETING——Persons appointed or elected according to law, authorized to manage and direct the affairs of a corporation or company. The whole of the directors collectively form the board of directors. When they meet, they have a Directors Meeting.

DUE DILIGENCE——Such a measure of prudence, activity or assiduity, as is properly to be expected from, and ordinarily exercised by, a reasonable and prudent man under the particular circumstances.

EMBOSS——To raise in relief from a surface.

FLIPPING——Buying and selling quickly for a profit.

FOIL STAMP——Pressing very thin metal to provide decorative covering.

GENERAL PARTNER——A partner of a partnership in which the parties carry on all their trade and business, what ever it may be, for the joint benefit and profit of all the parties concerned, whether the capital stock be limited or not, or the contributions thereto be equal or unequal.

'HOT' STOCK——An underwriting of common stock of a corporation that is in such great demand that the price is expected to immediately rise above the offering price.

LIMITED PARTNER——A partner in a partnership consisting of one or more general partners, jointly and severally responsible as ordinary partners, and by whom the business is conducted, and one or more special partners, contributing in cash payments a specific sum as capital to the common stock, and who are not liable for the debts of the partnership beyond the funds so contributed.

LITIGATE——To bring into or engage in litigation, the act of carrying on a suit in a law court.

LITIGATION——Contest in a court of justice for the purpose of enforcing a right.

MUNICIPAL BONDS——Debt issued by a municipality.

OPTION——A privilege existing in one person, for which he has paid money, which gives him the right to buy certain merchandise or certain specified securities from another person, if he chooses, at any time within an agreed period, at a fixed price, or to sell such property to such other person at an agreed price and time.

PLAT MAP——A map, or representation on paper, of a piece of land subdivided into lots, with streets, alleys, etc., usually drawn to a scale.

PREFERRED STOCK——A separate portion or class of the stock of a corporation, which is accorded, by the charter or by-laws, a preference or priority in respect to dividends, over the remainder of the stock of the corporation, which in that case is called COMMON STOCK.

SHORT SALE——A contract for sale of shares of stock which the seller does not own, or certificates for which are not within his control, so as to be available for delivery at the time when, under rules of the exchange, delivery must be made.

SPOILERS——A long narrow hinged or retractable plate that extends along the upper surface of an airplane wing and that may be raised above the surface for reducing the lift of the wing and increasing its drag.

STAT——A one step photographic process (versus a 2 step film and processing print).

STOCKHOLDER——A person who owns shares of stock in a corporation or joint-stock company.

STOCKHOLDER MEETING——A meeting of stockholders (usually annually) as required by the charter or bylaws of the corporation.

SUBPOENA——A process to cause a witness to appear and give testimony, commanding him to lay aside all pretenses and excuses and appear before a court or magistrate therein named at a time therein mentioned to testify for the party named under a penalty therein mentioned.

VELOX——A contact print from a photographic film. Velox paper was made by Kodak in the 1970s–1980s.

UNDERWRITING——The process of a contract, aside from its use in insurance, is an agreement, made before corporate shares are brought before the public, that in the event of the public not taking all of the shares or the number mentioned in the agreement, the underwriter will take the shares which the public do not want.